WAY OF THE STOIC:

LIFE LESSONS FROM STOICISM TO STRENGTHEN YOUR CHARACTER, BUILD MENTAL TOUGHNESS, EMOTIONAL RESILIENCE, MINDSET, SELF-DISCIPLINE & WISDOM

THOMAS SWAIN

© **Copyright 2022 – Thomas Swain.**

All rights reserved.

The content contained within this book may not be reproduced, duplicated, or transmitted without direct written permission from the author or the publisher.

Under no circumstances will any blame or legal responsibility be held against the publisher, or author, for any damages, reparation, or monetary loss due to the information contained within this book, either directly or indirectly.

Legal Notice:

This book is copyright protected. It is only for personal use. You cannot amend, distribute, sell, use, quote, or paraphrase any part, or the content within this book, without the consent of the author or publisher.

Disclaimer Notice:

Please note the information contained within this document is for educational and entertainment purposes only. All effort has been executed to present accurate, up-to-date, reliable, complete information. No warranties of any kind are declared or implied. Readers acknowledge that the author is not engaged in the rendering of legal, financial, medical, or professional advice. The content within this book has been derived from various sources. Please consult a licensed professional before attempting any techniques outlined in this book.

By reading this document, the reader agrees that under no circumstances is the author responsible for any losses, direct or indirect, that are incurred as a result of the use of the information contained within this document, including, but not limited to, errors, omissions, or inaccuracies.

Start Your Week The Right Way

We've all had that sinking feeling on a Sunday night, when you remember it's Monday tomorrow and the weekend is over. It can be tricky trying to launch ourselves back into work-mode, but with the right motivation and mentality, you can get your week off to the perfect start.

Receive evidence-based guidance, up-to-date resources, and first-hand accounts to help you.

Sign Up Now & You will receive this newsletter every Monday.

https://www.subscribepage.com/tswain

Scan the QR code to join.

CONTENTS

INTRODUCTION 1
THE GOLDEN AGE 11
  Who Were the Ancient Stoics? 13
    Zeno of Citium 13
    Marcus Aurelius 14
    Seneca 16
    Epictetus 17
THE FOUNDATIONS 20
  Oikeiôsis 21
  The Happiness Triangle 24
    Eudaimonia 24
    Live with Areté 25
    Focus on what you control 29
    Take responsibility 30
THE PATHWAY TO HAPPINESS 33
  Wisdom 36
  Justice 37
  Courage 38
  Moderation 40

Living Virtuously 42

THE DICHOTOMY OF CONTROL & ACCEPTING YOUR FATE 48

Amor Fati (love of fate) 52

SOCIETY, RELATIONSHIPS & LOVE .. 60

Relationships 66

Friendship 66

Love & Lust 68

THE PATHWAY TO SELF MASTERY ... 74

Apatheia 76

Discipline 82

Delayed gratification 87

HOW TO MASTER & CONTROL YOUR EMOTIONS 92

Stimulus, Perception & Response 98

Stimulus & The Discipline of Desire 101

Perception & The Discipline of Assent . 106

Response & The Discipline of Action 110

SHARPENING THE SWORD 113

The Toxic Emotion of Stress 116

Laugh often 121

See obstacles as opportunities 122

Mindfulness 125

- The Toxic Emotion of Anger.......................126
  - Let time pass................................131
  - Question you thoughts..........................132
  - See yourself as the offender...................133
- The Toxic Emotion of Jealousy..................136
- The Toxic Emotion of Envy......................139

THE POWER OF NEGATIVE THINKING 146
- Premeditatio Malorum..............................147
- Practicing misfortune..............................152
- Memento Mori....................................156

PRINCIPLES FOR INNER PEACE & HAPPINESS..161
- Gratitude..164
  - Practicing gratitude............................167
- Journaling......................................168

CONCLUSION..............................174
REFERENCES............................. cxc
OTHER BOOKS BY THOMAS SWAIN 195

INTRODUCTION

In the pursuit of living a better life how many self-help books have you read? How many inspirational / motivational YouTube videos have you watched? Countless I imagine. Just like me you've probably read or watched all too many. You see it's easy to get caught up in the trap of thinking that more knowledge is the answer. But in seeking answers we often become lost in the endless stream of self-help books, gurus, videos and motivational quotes that pop up every day. Yet rarely do they stick. In fact, many are recyclable and easily forgotten. New self-help fads come and go whilst the underlying issues still persist.

For many of us we feel like our life isn't anything special because it doesn't match the ideal standards portrayed in the media. Illusions persist of the ideal life being a series of highs. That life is about how much money you have in the bank. That life is about how flash your lifestyle is or about how much you own. Or how hot you are, or the social circles you move in. Additionally, we are now judged by how many friends we have on social media or by how many people view our stories, the number of comments or likes we receive and so on. People are always chasing these highs. Yet we see countless celebrities with large followings and a seemingly perfect life who seek mental help or in even worse cases have committed suicide. Is all that money, fame and glamor the source of happiness?

According to Stoicism the beliefs we hold and

the actions we take come from our descriptions of the world around us. All too often we value things which really aren't bringing us true happiness. Now this is all part of being human and we are still the same biological humans we were two thousand years ago when Stoicism first originated. We still face the same problems, emotions and adversities. Which is why Stoicism has lasted for thousands of years. It is a timeless philosophy which was originally developed to guide people to live their best lives. The basis of which is to live in alignment with nature. Essentially this means to act for the greater good of humanity because according to Stoicism all humans are connected through the universe and God is in all of us.

Now more than ever society has become fragmented and disconnected. So many people live in isolation, spending their days working in front of a screen and their evenings alone. Too often we think we are separate from the world.

Yet we are very much a part of it. However, the more we isolate the less happy we become because we are separated from the interconnectedness of our universe. When one considers themselves in isolation from our universe is when one does harm. When one realizes they are part of the universe they are living in alignment with nature. Goodness comes from understanding our place in the universe and collaborating with it for mutual benefit. This is the foundation of Stoicism which is living virtuously. Happiness is a by-product of this way of living.

Stoicism is often misunderstood as being uncaring or avoiding any pleasures. Or that it requires you to be unemotional with repressed feelings. Perhaps this misunderstanding has stopped you and many others from learning more about it. However, this is a false judgment which comes from Stoic ideas that teach us to not get carried away with irrational desires, pleasures and fears. Stoics are not stone-cold people without feelings. Incidentally in a study of more than five hundred Stoic students observed by the Modern Stoicism organization satisfaction with life and positive emotions both increased significantly through their practices.

Indeed, feelings and emotions are all a normal part of the human experience. It's not about pretending they don't exist. We can still feel them, cry or be happy and really experience those emotions. But Stoicism teaches us to not let them cloud our rational choices of what's best for our true nature. Much of the emotions and feelings that arise in us are automatic. We can do nothing about them. But we can accept them, and we do not need to act because of them. That's the difference between humans and animals. Animals act on their feelings whilst humans have the power of rational thinking. Stoicism says we should become conscious of our emotions. In doing so we can choose to not act emotionally but instead with reason. Consequently, we can choose the best way to respond to our emotions. When faced with fear or anxiety we will have the courage to act on what is best. When faced with temptation we will have the strength to do what is right.

Stoicism is a simple and easy to understand philosophy. Yet it is so profound. You won't need to learn a bunch of philosophy or to meditate for hours on end to understand it. Neither is it a religion. What we learn from it we are not called to follow. It is up to us how we apply it to our life and how much of it we utilize. The Stoics believed there is a divine force within the cosmos that exists beyond the reach of our human senses. They called this the Logos which is the divine reason implicit in the universe and "moves through all creation". Refusing the Logos is the root of suffering. Although their vision of God is not as a physical entity. It is instead perceived as a system of order and logic.

As such Stoicism can be adapted to align with other religions whatever your beliefs may be.

Living the way of Stoicism will require a revolution in your ways of thinking and attitudes. The Stoic philosopher must abandon their ego and existing view of reality to instead see life from a more universal view. One must dig deep into the soul to redirect their external life and to in turn become happier. Often this requires a reversal of one's thinking. Our values get reassessed to be not on externals but to be from the perspective of nature. False beliefs in finding happiness in materialism or status will need to be redirected. Because when we prioritize the external ahead of virtue, we are separating our nature from the universe which connects us all. When this happens, toxic emotions come up and we become more isolated. Instead, we need to realize that happiness comes from virtuous living. Good or evil is not contained in what we desire or avoid but rather it is in our thinking and beliefs. Any decisions and actions we take are based on those beliefs.

The principles of Stoicism are powerful and useful. That's why they have stood the test of time and are still applicable to this day. For me they have helped give purpose, meaning and direction to my life. I am Thomas Swain, a bestselling author and brand manager of History Brought Alive. I promise you that through Stoicism you can attain inner peace, overcome adversity, become aware of your impulses and learn how to respond in the correct way. You will learn to appreciate what you have, to find true joy and happiness in life. One can learn to manage negative situations of loss, depressing thoughts and even face your fears. You will see that happiness can come from the smallest things. When we break free from our attachments. When we let go of outcomes. When we learn how to control our emotions and take the right pathway, we can enjoy the deepest ocean of happiness.

Maybe you're lost right now, and you are seeking more meaning. Or maybe you're going through a rough time. Stoicism can help you. Whether you are a student, executive or just a curious person it will teach you to live your best life. Questions of how to live your best life will be answered. Questions of how to deal with what life throws at you will be dealt with. Along with dealing with desires and much, much more. You will learn to make better decisions based on logic and experience. This will help you in your career, studies and personal life. Ultimately it will guide you to a better life. The result is wisdom, inner tranquility and peace. In turn you will be more at ease with yourself whatever your past experiences are.

The future is better with Stoicism because you

can improve your overall life experience. Negative emotions can be effectively dealt with using its ancient and proven strategies from the greatest legends of history. A strong mindset is a key, and you will find how in this book. Not only can it help us in rough patches or crises, but it will also help us to cultivate a strong character with a clear head to deal with life and any rough patches or crises that occur. In the modern world it will help to improve your state of mind and in turn your overall life. Without a life philosophy to guide us we succumb to the whims of others and to the turmoil of life. Stoicism is the best life philosophy out there. Again, it is one that has stood the test of time for thousands of years.

THE GOLDEN AGE

Zeno of Citium was the first person to introduce Stoicism to Athens circa 300 BC. A student of Plato's Academy, he was first inspired by early ancient Greek philosophy which he later developed into early Stoic philosophy. Some years later his ideas were further developed by philosophers in ancient Greece and then by the Roman Stoics. Famous philosophers, Seneca, Epictetus and the Roman Emperor Marcus Aurelius can be credited with developing Stoicism. This was the golden age of Stoicism and it lasted for about one hundred years. In later centuries changes in culture and politics shifted away from philosophical thinking. Stoicism remained largely forgotten about until a modern-day revival.

In the beginning Stoicism was a system of complicated ideas involving logic, physics, grammar, meteorology and so on. Early Stoic philosophers focused on cosmic order and nature. The Roman Stoics later developed these ideas into ways of better living. Back then society was evolving, and people wanted to live a better life. One didn't assume that attaining prestige, wealth or beauty would necessarily bring them happiness. People wanted something more meaningful and coming from a deeper place. Increasing life satisfaction through ways of thinking and behavior was a keyway to improve their life appreciation. Stoicism provided the answers to stress, fear, anxiety and the trials of the human condition.

Who Were the Ancient Stoics?

Even though it started many years ago Stoicism has lasted until this day which is testament to its value. Throughout history there have been numerous famous Stoic philosophers but here we will explore the most important ones from those ancient times.

Zeno of Citium

Zeno of Citium is attributed with starting Stoicism. By all accounts he was a wealthy trader. During one of his sea voyages his ship was wrecked and he lost all of the cargo. Later on in life he realized that his perceived bad fortune of being shipwrecked had actually become something much more fortunate. With no boat or money, he ended up in Athens where he discovered the philosophy of Socrates and Plato. Inspired by their teachings he developed their philosophies into early Stoicism.

Zeno began teaching Stoicism at the Ancient Agora of Athens where he founded one of the leading philosophical schools of the time. Much of what we know about him is from the book, Lives and Opinions of Eminent Philosophers by Diogenes Laertius. Indeed, Stoicism has developed a lot since he began to outline the philosophy, but the fundamentals have stayed the same. As he would say "happiness is a good flow of life." That is achieved through the peace of mind which is the result of living a life of virtue in alignment with reason and nature.

Marcus Aurelius

Marcus Aurelius The Roman Emperor is probably one of the most famous Stoics from history. Born almost two thousand years ago into a prestigious family he would later become emperor of Rome which he led for almost two decades. During his reign he experienced wars with the Parthian Empire and many other attacks on the Empire. Furthermore, he was in the midst of the rise of Christianity, a plague that left many dead and much more turmoil during his reign.

Marcus left behind a personal diary which we now all know as his Meditations. Inside are the private thoughts of the most powerful man in the world at that time. Meditations reveals his own personal philosophy and brand of Stoicism. In his writing he explores how to be more virtuous, just, wiser and immune to temptation. It is a defining book on building character, self-discipline, ethics, self-actualization, humility, and strength. Naturally being a Roman Emperor during that time would have been a great position of prestige to be in. If he wished to, he could do or have almost anything. Essentially any desire could be satisfied, and nothing was off limits to an emperor. Yet he proved to be a noble and worthy man of his position.

"Waste no more time arguing what a good man should be. Be one." - Marcus Aurelius

Seneca

Seneca was born in the south of Spain over two thousand years ago. Educated in Rome he was the son of Seneca the Elder, a prestigious Roman writer. Seneca started out his career in politics and rose to become a top financial clerk. Later in life he experienced a changing of fortunes when Claudius, the new emperor of Rome accused him of adultery with his niece. Seneca was exiled to the island of Corsica. After eight years of exile, Agrippina, the wife of Claudius, negotiated permission for him to return and tutor her son Nero. Nero would later become one of the most infamous and tyrannical emperors in the history of Rome. Seneca was by his side as an advisor to help run the government and affairs of the state. However, as Nero became more paranoid their relationship declined and Seneca's eventual death came by the orders of Nero himself.

Throughout all of those turbulent times in Seneca's life Stoicism was the constant. His collection of letters is one of the most well-known works from Stoic philosophy. Inside can be found ways to conduct oneself, relationships, live a good life, approach adversity or death, and develop awareness of one's emotions. It is accessible for men and women from all backgrounds and walks of life.

"We are not given a short life, but we make it short, and we are not ill-supplied but wasteful of it." - Seneca.

Epictetus

Born a slave to a wealthy household Epictetus would later rise to become a famous Stoic philosopher. Mistreatment during his time as a slave had left him crippled and walking with a limp. His suffering motivated him to develop key concepts in Stoicism. Later on in life he was granted his freedom and began teaching philosophy in Rome, where he continued to teach for over twenty years. During this time, he was a major influence on Marcus Aurelius along with many other powerful men and women. Eventually his teaching in Rome ended when the emperor Domitian famously banned all philosophers there. Consequently, Epictetus relocated to Nicopolis in Greece where he established a school of philosophy which he taught at until his last days.

Many people throughout history and to this day find comfort in the ancient lessons of Epictetus. They draw strength from knowing that whatever is done to them is outside their control but at the same time they always have control over their mind. No one can take this away. Epictetus's Stoic philosophy was not only theoretical but also had real world, practical application to people from all backgrounds and walks of life. Yet he never actually wrote anything down. Arrian, his student, is to thank for the written accounts we have of his lessons.

"To make the best of what is in our power and take the rest as it occurs." - Epictetus

THE FOUNDATIONS

At the center of Stoicism is a universe which guides and connects us all to each other. The universe is vast and infinite. From the landscape to the earth, to the stars and the sky. It is all encompassing and includes all living things. We are all connected through it. Any imperfection comes from a misunderstanding of its parts which includes the humans who inhabit it. When one considers themselves in isolation from our universe is when one does harm. When one realizes they are part of the universe they are living in alignment with nature. Goodness comes from understanding our place in the universe and collaborating with it for mutual benefit. This is the foundation of Stoicism.

Nature in Stoicism is the measure of all things. It gives us guidance as a pathway to excellence. Through nature we develop reason and that transforms our understanding of ourselves. Zeno taught his students that we all have an inner genius and purpose which connects us to the universe. God is in all things and shares his divinity through all of it. The premise of living in alignment with nature concerns behaving as a rational human being rather than behaving out of passion as a wild beast would. Rational is what separates us from other animals. Applying our ability to reason towards our actions ensures that we live in alignment with nature.

Oikeiôsis

The Stoics developed the theory of "Oikeiôsis", to explain how reason transforms the world view of humans. According to this theory humans have two stages of development. The first is our initial impulse of self-love. In fact, all living organisms share this impulse. Whilst some are indeed more primitive the theory states that the first impulse is the awareness of a living organism recognizing that its body belongs to itself. As a result, it is compelled to preserve itself by pursuing things that improve its well-being whilst avoiding those that don't. For example, a plant grows towards sunlight. A baby craves milk and so on. Literally, it concerns the process of making something one's own. Everything in nature has its own set of responsibilities and unique character. For example, an animal must care for its offspring otherwise it neglects its duties of living in alignment with nature. This is actualized in its displays of making self-preservation its main goal. Whilst for human beings living in alignment with nature is something much more complex because we have the capacity for reason.

As humans grow, they continue to love themself and then through adolescence their ability for reason begins to evolve. From birth children are biologically wired to preserve themselves. Their motivation is towards pleasure and away from pain. As we age, we expand our consciousness to being a son or daughter, sister or brother, friend, citizen and so on. Essentially our biology extends to wanting to preserve this expansion because we now have a duty or obligation to them. Parents, siblings and friends are treated with care as an extension of oneself. Oikeiosis expands out into the human race albeit in an increasingly diluted measure. Our natural Oikeiosis towards others is the foundation of how well we integrate into the universe. It is our affinity with the entire human race and the universe itself. The final stage which is the goal of Stoicism is to live in alignment with nature.

The Happiness Triangle

Living in alignment with nature for Stoics is the most well-known definition of living the good life. But what exactly does it mean? Ultimately the goal of life according to Stoicism is Eudaimonia. In Greek this means to flourish. Essentially it is the full attainment of happiness or living the good life. The happiness triangle is a simple and visual way of explaining this concept.

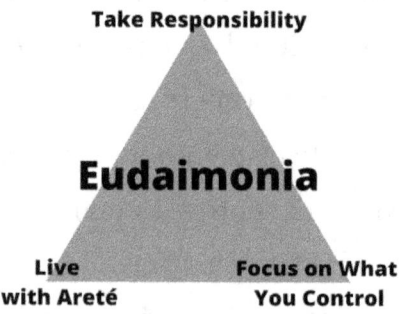

Eudaimonia

At the center of the triangle is Eudaimonia

which is the ultimate goal of life. In simple terms it is to have supreme happiness or to thrive. Achieving this comes through living in alignment with the other three parts of the Stoic Happiness Triangle. Which can be interpreted as living in alignment with nature.

Live with Areté

To live with Areté is to become the best version of yourself right now. According to Stoicism character and actions are more important than status or materialism. Stoicism welcomes everybody regardless of their background, circumstance or appearance. The real beauty of life comes from excellence of mind and character. Not the physical. Character is our only real possession. Everything else can be taken away.

Cultivating your character is the highest good. The ideal character is someone who lives in harmony with other humans and nature. They have serenity and follow reason. Whatever fate comes to them they accept graciously and realize it is beyond their control. They rise above desire and emotion to achieve peace of mind. Death is not something they fear. They are honorable, have strong self-discipline, wisdom, justice and courage. Continually asking questions of yourself can help you to live this way. For example:

- What is the right thing to do here?
- What would the perfect friend, father or brother do?
- How can I be my best at this moment?
- If I were developed to my maximum potential and living my best life, how would it look? Am I living up to that?
- What is the gap between who I am now and my best self?

- How can I close that gap?

We must make the time to work on improving ourselves and becoming better. As you become better you will lift up those around you and ultimately make the world a better place. That's not about being selfish. Afterall improving yourself is about transcending desire and serving others. Life is larger than the individual. In order to become our happiest and to thrive in life we need to express the best version of ourselves in each and every moment. Align with your deep values and act accordingly.

Stoicism focuses on not pointing out the faults of others but rather of improving our own faults for the benefit of others. As a result, we learn how to think better, to better prepare for challenges, to live more virtuously and to remove toxicity. We must be on a pathway of continuous improvement. There is always a deeper work going on within ourselves. Throughout the challenges and setbacks of life we should always be improving. Progress in life brings stability to us and as a by-product it benefits those around us.

"A good character is the only guarantee of everlasting, carefree happiness." – Seneca

A good role model will help you to measure your character. Find people whose way of life matches their words and character. This is the kind of person who would be a great role model. Now you don't necessarily need to know them in person. It could be someone you know through books, videos and so on. It could even be an ancient Stoic like the great Seneca or the emperor Marcus Aurelius. Whoever it is they should be a person of high virtue and moral standing. Let them be your guardian. How would they react to such situations? How would they behave in your situation? It is important to note here that you don't compare yourself to them. We are all different. Simply let them guide you. Allow their influence to guide your decisions and for them to be your guardian.

"If a companion is dirty, his friends cannot help but get a little dirty too, no matter how clean they started out." - Epictetus

Focus on what you control

Focus on what you control, this is a prominent principle of Stoicism. Living a good life requires focusing on what we control and accepting the rest as it happens. We can't change some things, but we can change how we respond. Other people's opinions, our reputations, possessions and even our own body we cannot control. In order to live a good life, we must focus on the things we can control. When we try to control those things, we cannot, it leads to anxiety, stress and worry. Indeed, there are many things we cannot control. But there are many we do. Living with Areté is something we can control. The past or future we don't control. However, in the present moment we can focus on what we control and create our best life. William Irvine identified three levels of influence we have.

- High influence - the choices, judgments and actions we take
- Partial influence - our relationships, health, wealth and behaviors
- No influence - external circumstances

"Of things some are in our power, and others are not." - Epictetus

Take responsibility
You are responsible for yourself and that

includes your own happiness. Take responsibility for living your best life and achieving Eudaimonia. Take responsibility instead of blaming others or your circumstances. This will free you from being mentally enslaved to the opinions of others. No more being a victim. Because when we take responsibility for ourselves, we become more powerful. We choose how to react and decide on what things mean to us. As a result, we become less upset about what happens or what doesn't happen. You are the only one who has access to your own mind. No one else. Take responsibility for who you are and how you live one hundred percent. Taking responsibility for your life puts you at the cause and not the effect. Doing this changes your energy and puts you onto a higher vibration. It is that energy that affects our thoughts, actions and feelings. The higher those are the better.

When you find yourself in the face of a challenge

do you blame others, or do you take responsibility? Accept the situation as it is. Observe and see what is in your control and what is not. Accept what is not and then make the most of improving what you control. That is your responsibility. When you blame others, you hand over that responsibility along with your emotions to them. No improvement of oneself is possible from there. One becomes a victim of life. So, wouldn't it be better to be in control of your life? Indeed, this is possible when you take responsibility for it.

"If you want anything good, you must get it from yourself" - Epictetus

THE PATHWAY TO HAPPINESS

The Ancient Stoics believed that the pathway to true happiness can be found through virtue. A virtuous life is about excelling in our human nature. To be free of passions that disturb the soul and to have rational understanding of one's responsibilities. Pursuing a path of virtue involves taming our desires, impulses and aversions. Happiness and living a good life are byproducts of living virtuously. Virtue in Stoicism is distinguished as anything which contributes to happiness. Whilst vice is distinguished as anything which contributes to misery. Vice is ignorance whilst virtue is knowledge. Vice is dominated by strong and irrational emotions otherwise known as passions. Between virtue and vice is a gray area known as the indifferents. Now these aren't necessarily good nor bad, they are just preferred or dispreferred. The problem is that many of us misjudge indifferents and act contrary to nature. For example, when it comes to wealth. A person with bad judgment would be likely to act greedily and desire to be richer than is enough. In the process of attaining more riches they might neglect others and as such they act selfishly. Furthermore, if they lost their wealth then they would probably end up being more miserable.

Most of us associate happiness with the concept of having more. Whether that's more money, beauty, fame and so on we are led to believe it will make us happier. But Stoicism teaches us that less is in fact more. When we want more, we become a slave to our desires. When we want less, we can free ourselves from our desires. Sure, it's good to have possessions and to want more. A better house, a better car, more money and so on. We can appreciate the pursuit and acclaim of those. We should care for them, but we should not fear their loss because ultimately, they are indifferent. Happiness does not come from having more things. Even if we get all that we want it will still never be enough. Now don't mistake this conceptualization as being a person without feelings. No that is not the case. Instead, it is the ability to distinguish what brings true happiness and what does not. That is to understand the difference between virtue and vice.

- Virtue: Wisdom, Justice, Courage, Moderation.
- Vice: Foolishness, Injustice, Cowardice, Intemperance.
- Indifferents: Reputation, Beauty, Health, Wealth.

Wisdom

At the root of virtue is wisdom. It is the way of knowing what needs to be done and what must not be done. It is the knowledge of what is bad or good, or the knowledge of what brings true happiness. Such knowledge helps us to understand the world around us in a much more accurate way. Then we can make better judgments and decisions based on our experiences and knowledge. Those decisions shape how well we live according to nature.

Stoicism holds the belief that a wise man can be his own counsel and that anybody can make progress towards wisdom. Through wisdom we can discover more virtuous qualities including soundness of judgment, shrewdness, sensibleness and circumspection. The opposite of wisdom is ignorance.

"Without wisdom the mind is sick, and the body itself, however physically powerful, can only have the kind of strength that is found in a person in a demented or delirious state." - Seneca

Justice

Marcus Aurelius held justice as being the most important value. For him it was the source of the other values. Justice also known as morality is about doing what is the right and fair thing to do. Even in times of adversity or weakness. Our sense of justice dictates how we act towards others and how well we live in alignment with nature. Justice creates more fairness for everyone. It can be thought of as one's moral compass which helps us to focus not just on actions better for oneself but on actions that are better for us all.

Stoicism teaches us that we are all one and that

no one should harm another. That we are not born just to serve ourselves but for the common good of mankind. So that when we act for the common good it is justice being served. Are we acting respectfully, with kindness and fair treatment? Do we give or do we just take? When we damage the community, ultimately, we hurt ourselves. On the opposite side of justice would be doing wrong to another person, living in chaos and acting selfishly.

"What is not good for the beehive, cannot be good for the bees." - Marcus Aurelius

Courage

Courage stands at the opposite side of cowardice. It's about doing the right thing even when we are afraid to do it. One does their duty despite having any fear. Having courage helps us to overcome our weaknesses and to live virtuously. Those with courage still feel fear, anxiety and desire but it is courage that helps them to act in the right way despite their fears. Often our initial reaction when confronted with fear is to panic. Fear can take over our rational mind. But the courageous ones do not hold onto these initial reactions. Instead, they go beyond them.

Without persistence we are unable to endure any hardships on our way to a goal and as such we may give into sinful vices. Courage is not just about facing our fears it is also about having indifference to external situations. Ultimately courage will guide us to being able to do what's right in spite of any reservations and fears. Actualized courage can be seen as Marcus Aurelius struggling to overcome the corruptions of absolute power. To be a good man even whilst Rome was at the height of decadence and decline. It's about the fighter going out to battle in the face of fear. Each conquest requires courage and the process in turn builds more courage. Take action, take risks and gain the rewards.

"Two words should be committed to memory and obeyed, "persist and resist." - Epictetus

Moderation

Moderation is about knowing that real abundance comes from having only what is essential. When faced with temptation it helps us to defend against fleeting pleasures, pains and false realities. One is cautious about what they should and should not do in the face of desire. It is a way of knowing whether or not things are worthy of choosing or of avoiding. In modern times one might associate this with being mindful or of having moral consciousness.

Viewing matters in a detached way helps us to be more objective and to in turn do the right thing. In reality it can be actualized as controlling oneself from overindulging whether that be in eating, vices, thinking and so on. In turn we can benefit from long-term satisfaction over short-term fleeting pleasures. We can be free from materialism, extreme behavior, impulses, cravings and addictions. This helps us to thrive and live in abundance when we practice it correctly. Ultimately, it's about doing whatever is essential and necessary. Nothing more.

Stoicism teaches us to practice moderation in everything from wealth, appetite, indulgence and life. Especially these days in dopamine driven social media and life on demand we can benefit from it more than ever. We can stop ourselves from falling into the hands of greed, laziness and addictive behaviors. Through moderation we can attain more positive benefits including modesty, orderliness and self-mastery. The opposite of moderation is greed, addiction, instant gratification, laziness, and procrastination.

"Most of what we say and do is unnecessary. So, in every case one should prompt oneself: 'Is this, or is it not, something necessary?' - Marcus Aurelius

Living Virtuously

Early Stoics were taught to think clearly, make decisions with speed and to have no regret after deciding. Epictetus advised his students when making decisions to be mindful of what is in their control. First understand what it is you face. Is it under your control or not? Once you have determined what is in your control you can start to think clearly about it. Next determine if it is of virtue. Pass it through the four cardinal virtues. If it is something of virtue, then do it. Whilst if it is not, then don't do it. Really decisions can be that simple!

For anything indifferent, consider if they are preferred indifferents. This includes things such as good health, wealth, beauty, strength, reputation and so on. Whilst those dispreferred indifferents which are contrary to nature include things such as death, weakness, pain, disease, poverty and so on. In most cases it is better to avoid them but, in some cases, we have to stay virtuous and deal with them appropriately which would be to behave with indifference towards them. Realize that they are often temporary and do not affect our control of our inner being. The virtuous use of indifferents will lead to a happy life. Whilst using them wrongly will make one unhappy.

Take effective action. Only take action once you have assessed a situation. Take the time to think, plan and reflect before you dive into something. Consider the consequences, the pros and the cons. Good decisions depend on the time spent considering the right course of action. Obviously, you don't want to get bogged down in too much thinking but just make sure you have at least put in some thought before you act. Look before you leap so to say. For big decisions it's a good idea to have it all written down so your mind doesn't go in circles and can work more creatively.

When a person becomes an adult with reason, they have the ability to perform "appropriate acts." Stoicism defines an appropriate act as being "that which reason persuades one to do" or "that which when done admits of reasonable justification." Each action we take must be authentic to our moral integrity. That requires one to understand the actions he takes and the impact of them not being just on his life but within the universe. Most people act selfishly and do not conform to the laws of life as a whole with respect to all of the virtues. To help understand our actions we can lay them out on a scale from vicious to virtuous.

1. Actions against the appropriate act
   a. For example, neglecting one's family, not treating others with kindness, squandering wealth or health in the wrong circumstances.
2. Intermediate appropriate actions which although are proper conduct but are not consistent with all four virtues
   a. For example, people pleasing, doing something for the benefit of one collective but at the same time it negatively impacts others.
3. Perfect acts performed consistently with rational
   a. This is virtuous.

We are not born sinful or corrupt, but we are born with resources to thrive in life. All of us have the seeds of virtue within us and it is our responsibility to bring them out. Yes, we all have different starting points. Throughout life we will be presented with obstacles, distractions and bad situations but we have the choice on how we respond to them. Our inborn tools and efforts determine ultimately where we will go. Living according to these virtues is the goal of Stoicism and it is progress towards living in alignment with nature.

Choose to thrive and live happily by living virtuously. Virtue in itself is its own reward. It is not about doing something because it feels good. Rather it's about acting in alignment with nature to be virtuous. Putting the knowledge of these four virtues into practice is paramount. It will help you to know how to respond in various situations. Whatever that situation is. Whether it be a positive or negative situation, one can choose to respond with virtue. Ask yourself questions before taking any action and let the virtues of Stoicism reveal the answers for you. Through practicing virtue, you can achieve happiness, success, honor, praise, love and live in alignment with nature. In the end your happiness and quality of life that depend on it.

THE DICHOTOMY OF CONTROL & ACCEPTING YOUR FATE

The Dichotomy of Control is one of the most popular teachings of Stoicism. All things in life can be divided into what we control and what we do not control. Wisdom is knowing what we control and what we do not control. Realize that what we control is very limited. It would be foolish and narcissistic to assume that everything is within your control. Trying to control things which you cannot, will also drive you insane. Emotional suffering is the result of people placing too much importance on things beyond their control. Stress is unnecessarily caused because simply it is not possible to change those things. Attachment to them makes us a slave to them. When things don't go your way emotions can spiral out of control since they are attached to something you don't control. Ultimately the most important thing within your control is your inner world.

Modern psychology recognizes the value of understanding the boundaries between what we can and cannot control. Happiness is around forty percent dependent on what we can control. Whilst just ten to twenty percent comes from external circumstances. The remaining forty percent of one's happiness requirement is within us. Knowing this it's possible to work on significantly improving one's overall happiness even if you are naturally pessimistic.

Regardless of external circumstances anyone can indeed be happier. First of all, realize that there are things you can control and those that you cannot. Essentially our inner world is what we can control. The majority of things in this world are out of your control. You have no control over what kind of family you're born into. You cannot control the economy, diseases, the weather and so on. Ultimately, we don't control what happens to us or even to our own bodies. People will have their opinions and you cannot control those either. Everyone has their own unique opinion. Whilst some might think your amazing others will think much less of you. There isn't much you can do to change that opinion. However, you can choose to not let it affect you because your own internal reaction is within your control.

We cannot control this crazy world, but we can control how we respond to it. Remind yourself of this every day. Let go of emotional attachment to wanting things to happen a certain way. Waste no more time complaining about things you do not control or in trying to control them. Peace comes from accepting this and letting go of what we cannot control. Unhappiness comes from trying to control what we can't. Understanding this will help you to move through the world with ease. Changing ourselves is easier than trying to change the world. Be the change you want to see in the world. Understanding this will bring you strength and wisdom. When you try to control those things often it brings unhappiness. Instead focus on what you have control over which are your thoughts, judgements and actions.

The archer analogy in Stoic philosophy explains this well. The goal of the archer is to hit the target. Some things he has control over. For example, he has control over his choice of bow and arrow, his training, his aim and when to shoot. He can do his best with all of these elements. But whether or not he hits the target is ultimately out of his power. At any moment the wind could come and cause him to miss. He has to be willing to accept all of the possible outcomes. In doing so he has to accept that he has done his very best. The rest is up to the universe. Believe and always do your very best. Leave the rest to nature. If it is meant to be then it will be. All we can do is our best, let go of attachment to the result and to accept whatever happens.

"You have power over your mind-not outside events. Realize this and you will find strength."
– Marcus Aurelius

Amor Fati (love of fate)

Stoicism calls upon us to be responsible for ourselves and to learn to accept the way things are. For example, getting angry in traffic for taking too long will not help to speed things up. It already happened and you cannot control it. Accept it. Our perception of what happens to us is in our control. We can decide if something is good, bad or indifferent. Learn how to differentiate between them. Then focus on appropriate reactions and actions from you. That is where your true power is. When you understand what you can and control it allows you to focus energy on what matters which are your thoughts and actions.

The ancient Stoics were big believers in fate and the powers of divination. They called this Amor Fati which essentially means, the love of fate. We have to accept that what happens is beyond our control. When we learn to accept what happens we go beyond accepting whatever happens to loving whatever happens. Realize that something greater than you is controlling your fate. Realize that it might be a step towards something much more favorable for you. Love that. This is Amor Fati.

According to Stoicism everything that happens is already predetermined and Stoic ethics dictate that human happiness is caused by conforming with the predetermined plan. Otherwise known as living in alignment with nature or God's plan. However, they also argue that we all have countless different realities which depend on the choices we make and the paths we choose to follow. Our destinies are written but we have free will. If we live in alignment with nature, then we will realize our destiny which is to live our best life.

Now some of you might say that if our outcomes are already fixed then why bother? If it is already fated, what is the point? The Stoics would answer that sequences and events are co-fated. The big events in our lives such as the day we die and the day we are born are fated. It is our individual character which causes us to decline or to take the best actions presented to us. Socrates knew through a dream that he would die within captivity in three days' time. He chose to accept God's plan and to not resist it. If he were to act against nature maybe, he would have escaped. But regardless he would still have died in three days time. Choosing morality will align you with determinism. Within this framework we can make the right decisions and meet our best fate.

Outcomes still depend on your actions which you control. If you sit there and do nothing it won't bring you a good life. Stoicism requires you to take the right action. Remember it's not about being passive with no ambition. Thinking ahead and devising the best strategy for achieving what you want is necessary. Marcus Aurelius faced numerous plagues and many misfortunes outside of his control, but he prevailed. Otherwise, Rome would have fallen. Imagine the metaphor the Stoics often used of a dog moving along tied to a cart. The dog can enjoy the walk with the cart even though he is not in control of it or he can resist it and be dragged along by it. We too have the choice to accept our fate or to be dragged along by it. In both scenarios we end up at the same destination, but one has a worse experience than the other.

Stoics take action. They don't just sit there and think about living a good life. They go out there and practice it through taking the right actions. We must continue to move forwards towards our goals. We may expect a certain outcome, but we might get something much better. Focus on the process of taking action and enjoy the journey. This is within your control. When things go beyond our control, we still have the control of how to respond. Focus on doing your best. Stoicism teaches us to take action without thought for future rewards. There are three premises to taking action. One is to guard ourselves from acting out of impulse. Two is to be mindful of the actions we take. Then number three is to remain detached from the results of taking action. When it comes to the results, accept them for whatever they are. Ultimately events in the external world are beyond your control. It is therefore better to accept them as they come.

"Fate leads the willing, and drags along the reluctant," - Seneca

As Stoics we are supposed to do what is right and to do our best. We are also supposed to accept whatever happens. Seneca defined this as "I will sail across the ocean, if nothing prevents me." This is the key to building confidence and trust. Have faith that you know you have done your best and the result is out of your control. Accept the result whatever it is and continue to act in alliance with virtue. This is the process. Along the way you can adapt and change the plan when circumstances change. Everything that happens was meant to be. Keep moving forward and you will see that what you might think is bad will become good.

Nothing is more powerful in Stoicism than the realization of the dichotomy of control. Internalize your understanding of it because it will help you greatly in life. It is simple to understand but it can be difficult to practice. When we are going through tough times it can make things more manageable to remind ourselves of what we have control over. This takes our attention away from the perceived problem and focuses it onto what we do control. Letting go of the fantasy of being in control allows us to deal with life much more effectively. Everything that happens can be endured or not. Either endure it or stop complaining. Do not waste your time on things you do not control. Accept what comes your way and realize it is helping you to grow in the long run. We come again to Amor Fati which is the loving acceptance of one's fate.

SOCIETY, RELATIONSHIPS & LOVE

Thousands of years ago the ancient Stoics underlined the importance of not doing things only for personal gain but also for the common good of human society. At the time this was a poignant message in what was a corrupt society overrun with self-interest. Whatever walk of life we are from our actions can bring benefits to others. Exercising care and concern for the universe helps us to live our best lives. Caring for the universe means we also care for ourselves because we are all one. When humans think universally for the whole community and live according to the four cardinal virtues they are living in alignment with nature.

A unified rational self was one of the main beliefs of the Stoics and maintaining that unity was paramount to them. Blaming others would be a diversion from unity and that would be a mistake. This is how conflicts arise. Most of it is failing to have empathy or to understand another's point of view without judgment or false impressions. We must be in harmony with our universal nature. A golden Stoic rule is that "no man is an island". Realize that our own individual interests are intertwined with those interests and concerns of others. If we focus only on ourselves then we will suffer and fail because we are acting selfishly and against humanity. Stay connected with others and treat them as well as kindly you would yourself. Our personal development relies on being of service to others. Treat family as your own, friends as family, strangers as friends and so on. Bringing the circle of others' lives closer to our own brings us closer to living in alignment with nature.

The basis of Stoic 'philanthropy' is loving for the fellow humans of our universe. Remember that we were all created for one another. Realize that we are all part of a larger entity. Marcus Aurelius suggested that we see ourselves as a limb of a larger body. Let this guide your thoughts, actions and life. Realizing that we are all connected is virtuous and crucial to living a good life. Stoicism advocates that we expand ourselves to encompass others. As explained earlier they call this Oikeiôsis. Our goals should incorporate the greater good of humanity because that is virtuous. Undoubtedly this will lead us to more kindness.

Stoicism teaches us to act in service of others without seeking for gain, praise or recognition. Since we are all connected through the universe it is in our nature to act in such an altruistic way. Taking is insatiable to meet one's satisfaction but giving is limitless to how much satisfaction it can offer. Zeno the original Stoic philosopher underlined the importance of duty and obligation to our family and society as being of high importance. According to his teachings we should do good things for other people without desire for reward or praise. When we act for the common good of humanity it is also better for us. Do good for the sake of it and expect nothing in return. Virtue will be your reward.

Become better and lift the world up with you because the more you develop yourself the better you can serve society. Even though it can be difficult and challenging, ultimately it will bring you greater joy than selfish pursuits of passion. Now your contribution doesn't necessarily need to be of a grand gesture. It can be small things that help other people's lives. Think of it like random acts of daily kindness. Or charitable projects that you're involved in. Keep thinking about ways to improve the lives of others and the community. Always be on the lookout for how to make a difference. Be the shoulder to cry on. Be the friend who listens. Be kind and be of service. Help others when you see they are in need. Perhaps you can go out to volunteer or make a donation to charity. Take every opportunity to show your kindness. Make someone's day. Make a list of all the acts of kindness you do. From big to small. It could be something as small as a smile, a compliment or even holding the door open for someone. But remember to do it without seeking reward or praise. Do not brag about it or show off. Just do it for the simple act of being kind.

Indeed, it might seem somewhat overwhelming to be responsible for others whilst you struggle with your own personal responsibility. But simply it is about having responsibility for the greater good. To not act selfishly, to think of how your emotions and actions impact others. Doing the contrary is to go against nature which is not virtuous and will ultimately bring sadness and negativity. Aimlessly chasing your own desires and pleasures is a recipe for a lonely life and one that is without virtue. Serving others and making contributions to humanity are the keys to living a good life.

But what about when other people do you wrong? The ancient Stoics were of the belief that people do not act wrongly on purpose. They believed that people act in the way that they think is best for them. However sometimes they are not truly aware of what is right for them. Therefore, we should not blame them but rather we should have empathy for them. We are all born with a blank canvas. Throughout our lives we soak up information, emotions and experiences. Our brains map everything out and we start to become shaped by our environment and life. These culminate to make all of us very different and unique in our own ways. Indeed, some of us are raised in less favorable pathways.

Some of us experienced rough childhoods, bad situations, lifestyles and influences along our individual journeys. To understand each other we need to realize empathy and compassion. When we become more compassionate, we can relate with and understand each other much better. Ultimately it enhances our concept of unity with others because it helps us to understand them better. Stoics appreciate the differences of others to understand their values and beliefs. This is the power of empathy. To be able to deeply feel and understand another person.

"What brings no benefit to the hive brings none to the bee" - Marcus Aurelius

Relationships

Friendship
In Stoicism relationships based on natural

feelings are healthy and should be cultivated. But those based on passion, dependency or without reason should be avoided. Friendship was valued by them, but it was also understood that friendship comes with certain tensions. Indeed, they can be fulfilling but they can also lead to dependency. True friendship is only possible after taking out attachments wherein people are not just friends to gain something. Again, it's not about cutting ties from other humans and living in solitude. Just be aware that everything is fleeting, and nothing lasts forever. Don't get attached to or hold onto people. Such behavior is possessive, and it ultimately leads to misery. Embrace and accept that life is impermanent.

Remember that the people you surround yourself with are who you become like. When you're around them for long enough you will start to talk, think and act like them. Take careful consideration of who you associate with.

Choose people who want to be better humans. Who are ambitious and living the lives you aspire to? Or maybe they aren't successful now, but they have the motivation and drive to become better. Weigh carefully the people in your life. Surround yourself with great people and you too will become great because they will lift you up. Make sure they are people who you aspire to be like. Are the people you associate with lifting you up? Do they inspire you? Do you want to be like them? Yes, should be the answer here. Otherwise, it's time to meet some new people. In the end it's better to be alone than in bad company because keeping bad company is toxic.

Love & Lust

In modern society a great deal of importance has been placed on romance and love. Movies and media portray idealistic representations of romantic love. But some people live for it and the problem with that is that they are in pursuit.

Love we can give freely without expecting anything in return. But love is unnatural and unnecessary. Nature doesn't make us desire love but rather it is society that does. Love is an obsession to fulfill a desire. It might seem wonderful, but it often brings pain. Once a loved one is absent, one becomes obsessed with missing them.

Lust on the other hand is a desire which is out of our control. In states of lust, we crave for another person and that makes us a slave to that desire because we cannot control that other human. Now that doesn't mean we should completely try to abandon lust. For example, sex is a form of lust, and it is seen as a preferred indifferent. Meaning that it is natural, but it is also unnecessary. We do not have to avoid it, but we should be careful not to overwhelm ourselves or do wrong things because of it. For example, to not be impulsive which often leads to regret. The levelheaded Stoic realizes that sex can disturb one's mind when mishandled which can make them act incorrectly. However, they realize that sex is something humans will do anyway. Therefore, it should be arranged to produce the least pain and most joy possible.

When couples first fall in love, they get caught up in a period of infatuation otherwise known as "the honeymoon phase". Generally, this doesn't last for long and all too often during this phase couples neglect to see each other objectively. As such they usually are blindsided by significant flaws or compatibility issues. When the honeymoon phase wears off couples are left facing these flaws and or compatibility issues. This can be avoided by taking things more slowly and getting to understand a person's nature without getting caught up in lust, craving or neediness. Avoid that desire to want or cling to another person. Keep your life filled with other things and not just that attachment to the person.

When a couple goes beyond the honeymoon phase and stays together is when a lasting relationship begins to form. This is based on companionship, trust, honesty and friendship. One should only commit to someone if they meet those criteria. Stoicism teaches us to have healthy relationships without clinging or lust. For single people Stoicism teaches us to be as pure as possible before marriage. If one does choose to indulge in pleasures, then they should do so with respect for and not to hurt others. One can have everything in moderation. Again, behave as if you were at a banquet. If something is passed to you, take a portion of it. If it has not yet come to you then wait.

Incidentally many schools of Stoicism teach that monogamy is unnatural and not beneficial to being happy. They state that men in particular should focus on more than one partner so that they can avoid the psychological obsessions and traps of love. Now please don't misunderstand this as being misogynistic. Try to look at it objectively without any illusions. Essentially, it's about not clinging to a person because as you know they are not in your control. Tranquility of the soul depends upon releasing ourselves from attachments to objects or people. Polygamy releases one from attachment and this reduces feelings of possessiveness or jealousy.

When a couple is in a monogamous relationship there must be concern and companionship for each other. Through the good and the bad times, they must stand by each other. When one person seeks to fulfill their own interest with neglect for their partner then the relationship fails. Ultimately there is no guarantee a relationship will last forever. Like everything in life, it is impermanent. Stoicism thousands of years ago taught the concept of letting go. They called it the "art of acquiescence". Essentially it is about giving up certain things and assenting so that they can be what they are to become. This is not so easy to achieve. After all we are humans and naturally, we all can get attached. Again, it's about realizing things are outside of our control. Detach from that ego of wanting and having. Believe and do your best. Leave the rest in God's hands.

Love with honesty and mortality. Remember that the core of Stoicism is virtue. When people enter into a relationship, they have the potential to create virtue and eventually to raise virtuous children. Relationships can then become a way to fulfill lust and live in a virtuous way. They can be warm and happy with couples living together virtuously and in harmony with nature.

THE PATHWAY TO SELF MASTERY

Human desires stem from our evolution. We evolved because of our innate desires for food, reproduction and aversion to discomfort in order to survive. Many of our basic instincts are shared with animals and in fact they have served us well. Overtime our desires have evolved for social hierarchy, sexual intercourse and more. It is this added combination of human creativity and imagination that has led our desires astray to unhealthy passions, compulsions and obsessions. In excess they have become dysfunctional and threaten our wellbeing. Desire can cause us unnecessary pain.

Actualized this can be seen as a rational creature acting out of alignment with nature. Or more simply put a human acting as an animal.

In modern times advertising and marketing campaigns manipulate our desires to make us value and want things more. Our impulses are aroused to take advantage of our weaknesses for materialism, sex appeal, power and status. Stoicism was ahead of its times because they knew how easily humans could be led astray. They advocated that we need to constrain our human desire within reasonable boundaries. After all, their motto was to "live in alignment with nature." Now this doesn't mean to go back to our primal roots, nor to go and live in caves. Instead, it's about resisting desires which are excessive because going beyond your human natural limit often creates pain or conflict. Just take a look back through history and you will realize that many wars and conflicts were caused by people seeking more than what was necessary for their happiness.

Apatheia

Apatheia is the Stoic mind state free from emotional disturbance. In literal terms it translates to living without passions. Now it is not to be confused with the word apathy which is a negative term. Apatheia is a positive term. Confusion between the two leads to detachment from reality. Apatheia helps us to effectively manage our emotions through recognizing and accepting them. According to Stoicism it is the fundamental purpose of humans to find Apatheia. Now please don't confuse that to mean living without emotions. Emotions and passions are different. Passions are the result of desire whilst emotions are part of the normal human experience. In those days the words also had a different meaning from our modern terminology. The ancient Stoics did not aim for a passionless life nor one without emotion. Self-awareness is the key. Even modern psychology tells us not to hide our emotions but to be aware of them. This is how we can make real changes and in turn live virtuously. Again, contrary to misjudgments Stoicism is not about depriving yourself. All of the emotions are experienced by them, but they choose to make the right choices not based on them but rather to be based on virtue.

Value comes from how you use it, not just to have it. Yes, we should have some things. For sure we need the essentials to live a comfortable life and we should always strive to improve our lives. We don't need to eliminate our desires completely. Commonly people come to Stoicism and assume they need to give up all their pleasures and vices. They think it will require them to give up things such as alcohol, drugs, sex and so on in the pursuit of happiness. They think that Stoicism forbids its followers from indulging in pleasures. Pleasure is not something we are forbidden from in Stoicism. No, you do not need to deprive yourself. We should still be inspired by beauty, to enjoy eating delicious food, to have fun with friends and so on.

A well-trained Stoic may for example may see someone attractive and feel a flicker of desire. Of course, this is a natural response. But that is not lust. Lust happens when someone imagines intimate relations with a person. They are consumed by the feeling and associate it as being good rather than what it really is which is indifferent. We think these things are inherently good but ultimately, they are indifferent. In the same regard our fear of missing out or fearing dispreferred things such as poverty, loneliness, low status and so on are also indifferent. All of these are based upon false beliefs appearing as real. Seneca the famous Stoic philosopher said we should enjoy the pleasures that come to us, but we must remain indifferent to their absence or presence.

In Stoicism passions can be explained as giving assent to an impression. It is what comes after our automatic response to things. Those are beyond our control. This is the reasoning behind focusing on what is under our control. Freedom from our passions depends on releasing our emotional response to the events we don't control. Stoicism divides passions into healthy and unhealthy passions. A well-trained Stoic mind is able to know the difference. Ultimately, we need to learn to be happy with what we have. Be grateful and make the most of life. Focus on appreciating everything you have and cultivate having the right things. Not things to impress others or to distract us from our purpose.

Through Stoicism we can learn what truly makes us happy and realize how it affects us and what they truly are. A happy life involves pleasure, but it has to fit into the bigger picture and be clearly understood. Stoics state that you must follow virtue. Virtue is the guiding principle of Stoicism. It is the highest good and is a combination of the four qualities of wisdom, justice, courage and self-control. To truly experience pleasure, we must make virtue the ultimate pursuit. Through the pursuit of virtue, we will experience pleasure and happiness as by products. Make sure you follow that order of pursuit. Virtue is not something that can be faked. It is true and must be cultivated through real practice. If virtue is not there, then the pleasures of life will be hollow. You will be under their spell and dependent on them.

Remember Stoicism is not a religion that promises damnation to those who fail its teachings. Following it is not a requirement. But if you do, your life will certainly improve. The Stoics knew that after all we are humans. We are not perfect. We will get tempted, attached, upset and we will fail. All of that is fine. Realize, recognize and learn from it all. Reflect on it and analyze how to improve because you have to be constantly improving. With an understanding of human nature, we can seek joy instead of pleasure. We can be cautious instead of fearful. We can wish for the best rather than to desire it. We can avoid grief, jealousy, depression, anguish, and worry. When we trust in the cosmic nature, we can love the outcome. This trust presents good in all events that occur no matter how bad they might seem. With this attitude we can grow and realize new opportunities. Through Stoicism one learns to love whatever happens to them because it is for the greater good of the universe. Amor Fati. Life shapes us just like muscles are grown through discomfort. Consider your own challenges and how they have made you better. Ultimately this requires an assent to providence. Essentially that is to be guided by God.

"Wealth consists not in having great possessions, but in having few wants." – Epictetus

Discipline

Stoicism teaches us self-mastery through having self-control, responsibility, objectivity and self-examination. Without such discipline we would float through life and be at the whim of the world and our desires. Through discipline we can take charge of our lives. Whatever goals you have in life they will require work. Much of that work is about overcoming impulses and doing what's right even when you're tempted astray. Now that feeling of temptation doesn't necessarily disappear. But the more you act in spite of those impulses the stronger your discipline will become.

Epictetus said that we become free by removing desire not by filling our hearts with it. Longing or craving for something is a thing we share with animals, but we have the ability of reason to apply to our actions. Too many of us hope, crave and wish. We wish to meet the right partner, to lose weight and so on. But we often don't take enough action. We hold ourselves back. We can sit, pray and beg all we like but until we do something about it, our life will likely stay the same. Each of us has to take responsibility for ourselves, our thoughts and actions. Moving forward requires deliberate action. Not desire. It's ok to be intimidated by the obstacles you face. Don't wish for it to happen. Make it happen. Utilize discipline to overcome desires and take action.

Stoicism helps us to take the right course of actions and to have a strong willpower so that we do what is best for the universe. In the face of temptation this is useful because you're going to be tempted throughout life. Will you behave like an impulsive dog, or will you think before you act? Again, a Stoic is not someone lacking passion or emotion. They just know how to behave the right way. They know when enough is enough. As such they don't get lost in drugs, alcohol or addictions. Sure, they can indulge a little here and there but they know where the line is. That line is the difference between being controlled by something or being able to enjoy it on your own terms.

Discipline is one of the most important skills to mastering a successful life and overcoming unhealthy desires. When you master a part of your life it creates a positive feedback loop across the whole of your life. For example, getting your body in top form gives you more energy which leads to better productivity and business success. Or for example mastering your finances gives you more freedom to pursue your other goals. You get the picture. It's about mastering yourself so that you can live to your full potential. Always try your best at whatever you do. Never give less than one hundred percent. Often the reward is in the personal growth from the effort put in. Find what you're good at and go all in on it.

Many people think motivation is the key to getting things done. Indeed, it can get things done. Problem is that it comes and goes. Therefore, relying on it will not give you consistent results. That's where discipline comes in. When motivation is not there, discipline gets the job done. Realize that temptation and distraction make building discipline very hard. Emotions conflict with discipline because they affect our ability to resist temptation. In states of heightened emotions humans fail to be rational and they often engage in acts of immediate gratification, or they make bad decisions. Alcohol is a massive inhibitor here because it shuts down our logic.

Ultimately the worst decisions are made when under the influence or when one is in a negative emotional state. In order to make it easier to be disciplined, identify and remove those inhibitors to your success. Avoid situations that cause temptation. If you're on a diet, get rid of junk food in your house. If you struggle with alcohol, then replace the feeling of a drink in your hand with a glass of soda. Most people usually just like having a drink in their hand. If you struggle with lust, block porn sites, track your compulsions and so on. Find out what your temptations are and work on ways to avoid them. Hide away the junk food, turn your phone on silent, work standing up and so on. Keep practicing discipline and give those muscles a workout. Excessive comfort diminishes discipline. Practice things which require discipline. For example, waking up early, cold showers, exercise, reading and so on. Start small and keep going. Stack the wins. What you feed grows. Feed your mind with discipline. Indeed, it can be difficult to cultivate more discipline because we have to be responsible for our actions.

Delayed gratification

Good things come to those who wait. This is one of the most important principles of building wealth or in fact anything worthwhile. Incidentally all religions promote delayed gratification as being one of the highest virtues of humans. They realize that humans who resist short term temptation will usually benefit in the long term. Sacrificing today will increase your quality of life in the future. I like to think of it as doing a favor for my future self. I thought of this every day when I set aside a year to work two jobs and invest in my business. Now I can live well thanks to my past sacrifices. Thanks to my friend in the past. Whilst those small sacrifices I make today will help me in the future. You save money to live a better retirement. Or you say no to the extra drink to save your morning and future health.

Delaying gratification is powerful because the benefits of it compound into the future. For example, you save money, and it continues to grow. You don't eat that cake, so you save your future health. We spend years studying and it can give us a lifetime of work and financial rewards. We invest in quality relationships, and they can improve our life infinitely. All of this makes our life infinitely better going forwards. Arguably it is one of the most important traits of a successful life. Therefore, all of us should learn and practice how to delay gratification. So how do we develop delayed gratification?

Realize that those who struggle with delayed gratification usually lack self-control and are controlled by their emotions. They struggle to resist temptation and it bites them back eventually. I have met so many people who didn't know where to draw the line. They always stayed up late and overindulged at parties. It negatively impacted their life. They lost their jobs and had to move back to their parents because they didn't know when to stop. They overindulged, overspent, overate and it messed up their futures. I have witnessed this over and over again. People left broke or dependent on their families because they didn't prepare for the future. Because they didn't know where to draw the line or understand the concept of delaying gratification. Recently we have witnessed this happen to millions of people who were not ready for the pandemic. People had gotten so used to living in the moment. Spending all they have and when the pandemic hit, they were unprepared for it. Don't be like them! Learn how to delay gratification so that you can protect and promote your future. You will not be the one who goes out in a flash but instead someone who lives a long and prosperous life. Think of the turtle and the rabbit fable. The rabbit sprints the race and runs out of gas before the end.

Meanwhile the turtle catches up at a slow pace and wins with ease.

Remind yourself of why you're delaying gratification. Usually, we focus on the immediate benefits but in order to stop doing those things that hurt us we need to look at the big picture. For example, if finance is a problem for you then create a compelling vision of the life you want to live. Set goals. In fact, set big goals that compel you. Choose a big goal in your life that means something to you. The things you want to achieve in this life, year, month, day and so on. Get clear on those and have a written account. Create that strong vision. Everyday feel, see and hear it. Creating a vision board of your goals can help you to manifest them. Find images that represent your goals. Look at them day and night. Feel them, see them and hear them. Always think in the big picture. Have a long-term vision of success beyond immediate gratification. This will help you through the ups and the downs. Think of it like your stock market portfolio and watch it grow over the years. We should always be working towards something because it will keep us focused and driven towards succeeding. Stay accountable also by having someone to keep track of your challenges, achievements and so on. This will help you to build confidence and more resilience as you go onwards and upwards.

HOW TO MASTER & CONTROL YOUR EMOTIONS

Stoicism is often misjudged as the suppression of emotions. Really this is not true. Much like other humans, Stoics feel all of the emotions. Contrary to popular belief Stoicism does not advocate the absence of emotions. Instead, what it teaches is to gain mastery of our emotions so that we are not carried away by them. One will never be free from negative emotions, but one can learn to gain control over them. This isn't about denying or suppressing your natural emotions. No, it's about understanding those emotions and coming up with the most effective responses. To be free from false judgments and to align with the truth that sets you free. In turn this will make you an all-round, happier and better human.

According to Stoicism emotions are the excessive attachment to preferred indifferents. Emotions influence our approach to different situations. Each of us has our own unique emotional character. Optimistic people tend to make optimistic decisions whilst pessimists tend to make pessimistic decisions. The glass is either half full or half empty. Essentially, we view things in different ways based on our own unique emotional characteristics. Most of this is unconscious and that can cloud our rational judgment. Appetite, fear, pleasure and distress are the four main types of emotion. Fear and appetite are faulty judgements of things being good or bad. Whilst distress and pleasure are faulty judgements of things in the present. Within each of these are subcategories.

- Fear - the expectation of something bad happening. The soul shrinks and we experience agony, hesitation, dread, panic or terror.

- Distress - an irrational shrinking of the soul and the experience of emotions such as envy, malice, grief, pity, anguish, annoyance and so on.

- Appetite - when the soul irrationally stretches or swells in expectation of something good such as wanting, anger, craving, yearning and so on.

- Pleasure - heightened feelings towards what seems worthy such as self-gratification, rejoicing over another misfortune, enchantment and so on.

Emotions are powerful. They can cloud your judgment and cause you to act wrongly or to make mistakes. Just think back to your past. I'm sure you can recount many times where you got angry and said or did the wrong thing. Or maybe you misread a situation when your emotions led you astray. Losing control of your emotions often causes much more long term hurt. Recently I witnessed an enraged man kick and punch another person's car. Is that helping anyone? To me it looked like the behavior of a child. Such behavior could have landed him a night in jail or a big fine. Tantrums will not get us what we want in life. Realistically they are an immature management of emotions.

All of us have at one time or another done or said something foolish because of our emotional response. You get angry at the waiter for bringing food late. You get lazy and leave things to the last minute. It is these emotions that can cloud our rational minds. We like to think we are rational but for the most part we are not. Emotions are a subjective state of mind. They come from our bodily reactions to a stimulus and then we feel them in our heads. Fear makes us sweat and shake. Love makes our hearts beat faster. Our body registers an emotion first and therefore it is not possible for us to use conscious powers to stop emotions. However, we can use our conscious power to redirect our emotional states. After experiencing an uncomfortable reaction, we can control how we respond consciously to be better for the mutual benefit of the universe. This method is at the heart of many psychiatric therapies such as cognitive behavioral therapy in addition to ancient philosophies, like Buddhism. In an ideal world a person makes their rational decisions with little disturbance from emotions. For example, it rains and that changes your plans. Or you get stuck in traffic and it makes you late. How would you react? With anger? With frustration? Or would you act like a Stoic? A Stoic would not let their initial impressions carry them away. They would try to be objective and in turn choose the best response.

Mastery of your emotions will enable you to do the right thing even in the face of adversity. Stillness can be found in chaos with tranquility of mind regardless of the external situation. Imagine the commander in a war zone who must stay calm and not be overtaken by their emotions. Otherwise, it would be catastrophic.

Stoicism helps one to be more emotionally resilient in adversity. It offers the student a new way of viewing the world, a framework to manage it through and a philosophy for life. Emotional resilience is about being able to deal with stress without being overwhelmed by it. When we are faced with obstacles and challenges, we often become emotional. But the best way to overcome them is to keep our emotions in check and stay grounded. In staying grounded we are better prepared for the fluctuations of life. This is something we can all work on making stronger. Stoicism is synonymous with this mindset.

Stimulus, Perception & Response

When misfortune hits us, it can be difficult not to be swept away by autopilot reactions. Seneca taught that it is the unexpected challenges of life which are the most difficult to ascertain control over. However, there is a gap between when we experience something and our judgment of it. When something happens, you have the opportunity to pause and consider how you judge it and then to decide how to respond. For example, when someone gossips about you, initially it can cause shock or upset. Either you can choose to let that settle into resentment or you can choose to move on. Or for example when someone cuts you off in traffic. Naturally this angers most people. But you can choose to be overwhelmed by the feeling of anger or to let it pass.

Ultimately, we have the power of choice over our thoughts and actions. Of course, doing the right thing requires practice. Practicing Stoicism can help us to improve our thoughts. But it often takes many years. Recognize the power of your thoughts because they are what create your world. Literally they can change your physiology and external world. The ancient Stoics were well aware of the power of thought. They recognized we have the power to respond how we want. If you experience rejection, do you take it personally or do you take it as a learning curve? If your team wins or loses, do you get depressed or do you let it go? Remember it is you who has the choice.

Epictetus said that thought was the first step in how humans become upset or stressed. We make judgments of things as being either bad or good. Sometimes these judgments can be extreme. When you get angry at someone you are judging something they did as being bad. But it doesn't need to be that way. After thought comes impulse. This is the impulse to act in an automatic way. For example, shouting when we are angry. Epictetus uses the term differently. Instead, he says that impulses are the first step as to when we judge something as being good, bad or indifferent. Essentially, they are our value judgments or our desire to act. We judge things all the time and make decisions on how to act. All day, every day this happens, both quickly and slowly.

According to Stoicism there are three stages of emotion:

1. Stimulus: An experience that could be coming from the outside, people or even your internal thoughts. The thought itself, without endorsement - which is the

appearance of emotion. We can make use of the discipline of desire here.

2. Perception: Assent or endorsement of the thought - this is within our power to apply rational and take control of our emotions. Inside your mind the stimulus is processed. How you perceive it depends on your thoughts, beliefs and values. We can make use of the discipline of assent here.

3. Response: How you choose to respond. This also depends on your thoughts, beliefs and values. We can make use of the discipline of action here.

Stimulus & The Discipline of Desire

Biologically as humans we were all designed the same in the ways to which we react to stimulus. From the day we were born we have had primitive emotional programs that help to ensure our survival. As we grow our brain evolves to understand the patterns that threaten our survival. When a perceived threat is detected, an automatic response is initiated. This happens not just with threats but in a variety of situations. Through nature and nurture, we develop automatic responses. These are largely unconscious and oftentimes in the modern world they don't help us so much. Do not feel guilty for your initial feelings because they are involuntary. The Stoics called this "propatheiai", and it is completely normal. Think of it as nature's way of keeping you from harm.

Our initial impressions of stimuli are not subject to any discipline because we cannot control the impressions that present themselves to us. Only when we respond to those impressions is when we become responsible for them. For most of us we attempt to handle things at the last stage, which is the impulse to act. We see some delicious food, an attractive person, an expensive suit and so on. This is presented to us as being of value and we assent to triggering desire for it. Some of us may even fantasize over having it. In the end we want it more and this causes us to act on our impulses.

Wise people are also gripped by initial events as part of the human experience. There is no shame in that. But they look at what can be done and ask themself questions such as, is it really that bad? Or what can I do to improve it? We can make use of this process in various situations such as moments of danger, anger, shock, fear and so on. Essentially in the moments that cause sudden involuntary reactions. Allow yourself to first feel that initial primal instinct. Accept it and then make a conscious effort to see it objectively. Let me elaborate through a story.

Once upon a time a Stoic philosopher took his students to sail across the seas. Rough waves and weather rocked the boat violently on its journey. The men and women on board panicked at the fear of it sinking. In the moment the Stoic philosopher was also gripped by fear. He remained silent in the face of the storm. After the storm had passed one of the students asked the Stoic why he was afraid. Surely, he as a Stoic would be able to handle the fear. He responded that even a wise man is disturbed by terror and danger. However, he does not hold onto those emotions. Ultimately, he realizes that they are indifferent. The fool on the other hand is also overwhelmed by the fear but he yields to it. Whilst the wise man stays steadfast and acts appropriately and rationally. Even though he feels fear just the same as the fool he does not let the terror excite him or cause him to make a bad judgement. This treatment is true with all emotions in Stoicism.

The discipline of desire helps us to not let things spiral out of control. Practicing the discipline of desire requires practicing the cardinal virtues of temperance and courage. One must as Epictetus says, "endure and renounce". Through practice we can avoid irrational pleasures and aversions that in the short term feel good but in the long term hurt us. In order to practice the discipline of desire we must continue to live in alignment with universal nature as a whole. One must also accept their fate as inevitable. We talked about this earlier "Amor Fati" which is to love your fate. Caro of Utica, a famous Stoic hero exemplifies this. Through the deserts of Africa, he marched in an attempt to overthrow Julius Caesar. In the end he lost the civil war but became a legend because rather than submit to Julius Caesar he pulled out his own guts with his bare hands.

"Seek not for events to happen as you wish but wish events to happen as they do, and your life will go smoothly and serenely." - Enchiridion

Perception & The Discipline of Assent

From impulse comes a second response which is our conscious response. Remember that the wise man and the fool are separated by the space between stimulus and response. The fool is overcome by the stimulus and lacks the rationale to respond in the correct way. Whilst the wise man is able to look at it objectively which is what the discipline of assent is about. Essentially it is awareness of your inner world. Think of it like mindfulness.

Notice how you make value judgments all the time. These judgments influence the way you view the world around you. Of paramount importance to Stoics is the assessment of good or bad judgments. We associate value to various things when often they are indifferent to us. Essentially the labels we associate with external events and people are that way because we chose them to be. Yet labeling them is not necessary. In Stoicism everything is seen as an opportunity. There is no good or bad but only perception. So, what exactly is perception? In simple terms it is how one sees a situation or interprets and understands it. However, that perception often is not a true reflection of reality. For example, someone who was lied to by a man in a previous relationship might now perceive all men as being liars. But this just is not true reality. Indeed, there are some men who are liars but not all of them are.

When we make value judgments all too often, they are overly emotional because we are using emotional terminology. Don't allow yourself to do this. Instead try to describe the situation in a more factual and logical way. For example, instead of saying you missed your flight and describing how awful it was. Instead, you could say, I missed my flight and now I am booking a new one. Avoiding emotional language to describe the situation will help you to worry less and to be less overwhelmed by it. After all you cannot change what has happened, but you can change how it affects you.

Realize that those emotions and judgments come from your own internal creations. Nothing really needs to be perceived as being bad or even good. Ultimately that perception is your own choice. Stoicism teaches us to stop adding those value judgments so that we can think more accurately and clearly. Think of it as non-judgmental awareness to see the world exactly for what it is without distortion. Allow yourself to create a space between impression and judgment.

You must see things the way they truly are and be mindful of when you are thinking because it is the gateway to controlling your thoughts and emotions. View the world in an objective way without clouding it with judgment or lies. Self-awareness is crucial to ensure correct judgements and actions. Continually work on becoming more self-aware. Practice makes perfect. Through consistent internal monitoring one can apprehend in advance any early warning signs of unhealthy impressions or desires which could cause going against one's nature. With this in mind we can remain self-aware, calm and rational regardless of circumstances. Remember to focus on what you control, which is your emotions and actions. Everything else is going to play out as it will. Keep rolling with the punches and bouncing back stronger. Through practicing Stoicism one can improve their perceptions which in turn leads to a happier and healthier life.

"Do not seek for things to happen the way you want them to; rather, wish that what happens, happens the way it happens: then you will be happy." - Epictetus

Response & The Discipline of Action

Stoicism teaches us that we must be responsible for the way in which we respond to the world. Humans naturally learn behaviors from nature and nurture which form a pattern of responses. As a result, we frequently end up making automatic responses to situations based on our behaviors. Incidentally while it might seem optimal, not all of this automation helps us. Early Stoic philosophers were well aware of patterned behaviors and responses. To counter them they practiced self-awareness so that they could be more critical in their perceptions and opinions.

How you respond is ultimately your choice and this depends on your beliefs and character. Becoming aware of how you respond is very important because if it is left alone then destructive patterns can begin to form. Think of it like a house you need to clean every so often. We can get lost in life and end up just going through the motions. Take time to reflect on how you respond to situations. Could you improve upon those responses? Maybe you responded angrily to a challenge. Maybe you misinterpreted a relationship and missed out on a greater opportunity. Analyze and reflect on your triggers. Work on cultivating better responses.

When we change our beliefs, we can change our responses. Perhaps that's about being more open minded or less attached to an outcome. Align with cosmic nature, understand and accept your choice as a human. As the dichotomy of control states, there are things which we have within our control and things which are not. Within our control are our own internal choices, desires, aversions, motivations and opinions. Whilst outside of our control are the material, reputations and things not of our own doing.

The discipline of action is about harmonious living with all mankind and wishing them the best. Even when others may not wish the best for you. Ultimately you cannot control them, but you can control your own responses and actions. It is in your power of choice to act virtuously and to help others. When someone acts angrily you don't need to respond the same way they did or even to be offended by them. Simply accept who they are and don't let it affect you. Do your best to act with virtue and accept the actions of others with detachment. A good Stoic does their best to act virtuously whilst accepting they cannot control outcomes of their actions. Act purposefully and with virtue.

SHARPENING THE SWORD

Every day we are faced with obstacles that can overwhelm our emotions. Things take us by surprise, people can challenge and confront us. Indeed, life sucks sometimes and things can often go wrong. We all experience it and there is no way around this. However, too many of us are ignorant and oblivious of this fact. We think catastrophe would never happen to us. But when it comes along, we are destroyed by it.

In a letter to his friend Lucilius Seneca answered the question, why do many evils happen to good people? Seneca replied that the Gods who control the universe have a friendship with us. The Gods challenge us with trials to make us stronger. Seneca also goes on to say that there is no bad thing for a good person. A brave person stays balanced in the face of adversity; it hardly affects them. Strong people pick challenging circumstances to make themselves better. To sharpen their sword so to say. Seneca challenges his friend to stay prosperous throughout life without any mental distress. To stay calm in the face of challenge and adversity.

"He who has waged an unceasing strife with his misfortunes has gained a thicker skin by his sufferings" - Seneca

Ultimately everything is temporary. Throughout history people have overcome adversity and gone on to inspire the world. Muhammad Ali became champion of the world whilst faced with racism and being stripped of his titles. The world overcame tyrants in World War Two. Marcus Aurelius faced numerous invasions, plagues and adversities. There are so many countless examples from history. All of these people who faced adversity no doubt felt fear, depression and overwhelming negative emotions. Yet they stood up and thrived despite that. Stoicism can help us to do the same.

First of all, we have to realize that perception is the key. The way we perceive and understand what happens to us and the world around us makes a huge difference in our quality of life. We decide what our perception and understanding is. This can either hold us back or lift us up. Stoicism teaches us to see the external as neither good nor bad but as indifferent. Therefore, it is our judgment of the indifferent which matters to us. It is you who must take responsibility for your judgment.

There is what happens to us and the story we tell ourselves about the meaning. How you perceive different situations will determine how you feel about them. Consequently, this will influence the ways in which you act. When you feel it's impossible you give up? When you feel it's tough but manageable then you keep on going. Try taking yourself out of the equation. Get a birds eye view on it and make an objective rational decision. Realize that you have the power in your hands. Even though circumstances may be out of your control we can still control ourselves, the ways we think, our attitude, efforts and so on.

The Toxic Emotion of Stress

Zeno the founder of Stoicism lost everything he had in a shipwreck. Seneca was exiled and suffered numerous health problems. Marcus Aurelius reigned over an empire during plagues, wars, bankruptcy, flooding and numerous other problems. Epictetus was a slave for thirty years. Such stresses they all faced. Stress comes from hard times, uncertainty, failure and pain. All of which are a part of everyday life. All of us face stress but that doesn't mean we have to be stressed by it. Sometimes it can become so overwhelming and there is not much you can do about that. Except the way you decide on how to deal with it.

Marcus Aurelius chose not to feel harmed. He talked about releasing and discarding stress. His journals were filled with notes on escaping stress and learning not to let anger control him. Epictetus repeatedly taught his students to focus on what was in their control and to let go of everything else. Stress relief at its finest! Seneca wrote not to suffer before it is necessary, and that stress is optional. Even though we are being stressed we don't need to let it overwhelm us.

According to Stoicism stress is a reaction to our perception. We feel stressed when our perception fails to meet our expectations. The point is that all too often we suffer more in imagination than in reality. We worry about how bad things will be. We all go through tough times, and you can't escape that fact. But we don't need to suffer so much from thoughts of pain that never happened. When you for example have an injury, pain comes from the damage inflicted. But more suffering comes from the thoughts about it. Such thoughts are not facts, they are just thoughts in your head. True you are in pain, but you don't need to create vivid stories about it or wallow in unnecessary self-pity.

As Seneca advises "do not be unhappy before the crisis comes." When you feel stressed out, analyze the feeling. Where does it come from?

Dissect it. Consider whether you are bringing it on yourself. Cut it out before it grows. Adjust your expectations. When we expect too much it can leave us frustrated. Instead work on having more appropriate expectations. The more realistic they are, the better your experience will be. Furthermore, Epictetus said our main task in life is to identify and separate what one controls and what they do not. When you let go of worrying about what is not in your control it frees up your time and energy onto what you can control. This gives you a distinct advantage in stressful situations. When we are being more responsible and creative, stress is going to be reduced.

"You have power over your mind not outside events, realize this and you will find strength."
- Seneca

When we change our perception of our

environment, we can see the bigger picture which reduces our stress. Those small conflicts, disagreements and arguments seem so small in the grand scheme of things. When troubles come to you, stay focused on the bigger picture. Often what you think is a big deal is just a small thing. Zoom out and see it on a grand scale of your life in the world. The View from Above is an exercise which the ancient Stoics practiced visualizing how we are all connected through the universe. One imagines oneself high up in space looking down at planet Earth below. This shifts their point of view from a first person to a third person perspective. Essentially this is a psychological process known as cognitive distancing which involves separating your thoughts for yourself. Writing your thoughts down is another great way to do this because it brings thoughts out of your head and into the world. Again, this creates distance and separates us from them.

Try looking at yourself in the third person view. Reflect on your problems as a third person. For example, John is thinking., as if you are studying them. Shifting your perspective will help you to free up you're thinking. Furthermore, you could also imagine how other people would deal with your thoughts. For example, what would Seneca do?

Laugh often

Apparently, a famous Stoics, Chrysippus, died from laughing. What a way to go! The ancient Stoics believed humor was essential to living in a world marked with suffering and challenges. They believed we should have a lighter view of things so that we can easily move through the world. Science proves that laughter and humor release the happy chemicals of endorphins in the brain. Instead of being so serious, look on the bright side and try to find the humor in things. Cultivate your inputs. Stop watching so many shows and movies. Switch to something more lighthearted. Watch funny shows, make jokes and find the humor in every situation. After all, it will keep you happy and youthful.

"He who laughs has joy. The very soul must be happy and confident, lifted above every circumstance." - Seneca

See obstacles as opportunities

The ancient Stoics believed that within every obstacle was an opportunity. Regardless of how bad a situation may seem there is always an opportunity there. It could be a lesson to learn, just look for it. Every time you face an obstacle see it as an opportunity. Too many of us think of obstacles as preventing our happiness and stopping our pursuit of our goals. But instead, we can reframe them to be challenges. For example, when you get stuck in traffic see it as an opportunity to cultivate more patience. Or when you face setbacks see them as an opportunity to become stronger and more persistent.

Our world is always changing. We need to be ready for change. Ultimately, we have little control over what happens to us. However, we can decide upon our reaction to it. Maybe you adopt the mind state of a victim. You think, why did this happen to me? Instead, why not look for the opportunity? There is a famous story of a farmer whose son fell from a horse and broke his leg. People go on to say to the farmer things such as, "that must be so terrible". "Maybe" he replies. Soon after a war breaks out and all the young men are enlisted. Except his son because he is injured. Maybe it wasn't so terrible after all.

The next time you're challenged, try to apply the same way of thinking. What is the value in this? How is this good? Ultimately good can be found in any situation. Sometimes that means turning things upside down. A potentially bad situation becomes good and so on. For example, you were late for an appointment but maybe you missed something negative happening to you. Or someone is mean to you and things don't go your way. Maybe they are teaching you knew values or helping you to improve.

The only reason difficult situations become obstacles is because we choose to make them that way. Instead, we need to look at them in a new way. A way that envisions progress and opportunity. We have the choice to be blocked by our challenges or to fight them. To shrink or to grow. Ultimately this comes down to our perception. Is your glass half full or half empty? Remember that this is not about being naive to the bad things that happen. Yes, they do happen, but we should not bury our heads in the sand. We should fight forwards and keep going. Train your perceptions to look for opportunities. See adversity as a chance to grow and test you. Seek goals and challenges that will test and improve you. Remember to have no expectation or attachment to the outcome.

Mindfulness

Most stress comes from when the mind wanders to a place other than the present moment. When it latches onto fear of the future, regret of the past or gets lost in thought. Practice being mindful. Being mindful of emotions will help you to understand if they are helpful or not. Furthermore, this will help you to choose the best actions of virtue.

The present moment is all we have. Time continues to move and can never be pinpointed. When you try to pinpoint it, it becomes the past or the future. Neither exist yet all too often we try to live there. In doing so we sacrifice the present moment which is the only place we can truly live in. Living in alignment with nature requires us to live in the present. Keep yourself in the present moment and enjoy life to the fullest. The present moment is your life happening right now. Don't miss out on it. Work on cultivating more mindfulness through exercises such as yoga or meditation. Both of these focus on connecting with the present moment. Take time out each and every day to practice them. Learn more about them through YouTube, courses, books, workshops and home practice.

The Toxic Emotion of Anger

Seneca famously called anger "a temporary madness". In the state of anger, a person becomes unreasonable and lacks rational. Anger can quickly erupt like a volcano exploding, boiling over and creating chaos. It spreads like wildfire in people which is unique since emotions are rarely so contagious and collective.

Populations, companies, teams and collectives can become infected with anger. Imagine mob behavior when people work together in violence, chaos and disruption. Seemingly normal people wouldn't do such crazy things alone. Yet together they can cause havoc.

Emotionally it is one of the most intense feelings. One becomes almost unconscious under its spell. We often get angry over such trivial things. The traffic, the weather, the spilled milk and so on. Instead, realize that getting angry only makes things worse because we end up hurting ourselves or others more than the original event itself.

Anger takes us over and distorts us. It turns the calm into a raging monster. Our ability to reason is clouded when we are angry. This leads us to make bad decisions and actions because we are not being our normal rational self. As a result of this we end up doing more harm than what the anger caused. For example, someone gets cut off in traffic and they become violent. Or an argument rises into regretful things said. All of us are affected by anger regardless of background or personality type. Even the most gentle and peaceful people can be affected. In those moments of anger, we are blinded by the future consequences of our angry actions. We make bad decisions, behave recklessly and cause much more damage than the anger did.

The ancient Stoics studied anger in depth. They understood that it can be prevented once one realizes the faults of anger. First of all, realize that anger inflicts harm. Harm to yourself and harm to others. For those who think that anger makes them stronger then really, they are trapped by it. When we become angry, we become a slave of it because it makes us blind and causes us to make mistakes which we will likely later regret. Just think of those times when you were angry. You probably did or said something you later regretted. The majority of road accidents occur when people are angry. People are hurt, murdered and killed because of anger. How much of this could have been avoided if people learned to let go of anger? How many lives could have been saved? Or wars avoided?

Working towards an anger free life requires a tranquil mind. This should be your highest goal. Once you realize how destructive anger is you can work towards breaking any attachment to it. That's the start of your journey. Understand that anger is not beneficial. It won't help you or anyone else. In fact, it will only make things worse than what initially made you angry. Tranquility is a better strategy. Realize that civilness and gentleness are more human traits.

Now if you consider yourself to be someone who

has a hot temper then learn what triggers it and find ways to soothe it. Being mindful and taking notes will help you here. The next time you feel yourself getting angry. Ask yourself why. What caused it? Make a note of that mentally, verbally or write it down. Moving forward, try to avoid those situations that often make you angry. For example, if you see a que of people then come back later. If the news makes you angry, then avoid it.

Furthermore, make use of specific practices to calm the mind. Listen to music that is calming or go for walks to unwind. Have a workout routine to destress or take time out to meditate. Get lost in an art gallery. Set aside times for these periods where you practice calmness and letting go. We can weaken anger by consciously being aware of the costs of it. Don't let the small things arouse anger. Try to stay calm even in the midst of the storms. Cultivate this mindset through experience. Become aware of those things that usually make you angry and try to stay calm during those times.

"Anger, if not restrained, is frequently more hurtful to us than the injury that provokes it" - *Seneca*

Here are some more points of wisdom from Seneca on dealing with anger:

Let time pass
Seneca advised that the greatest solution for anger was to let time pass so that the initial passion could die down. Simply waiting for some time to pass is a great way to calm the flames of anger. Emotions are transient and never last forever. Knowing this we can simply wait for anger to pass. Time and distance are the best solutions. The further away we are from anger the stronger we become. Interrupt the

pathway of anger with time. Take fifty deep breaths, count to one hundred backwards or repeat the alphabet during those times.

Question you thoughts

We can easily get carried away by our thoughts. Therefore, we have to question if those thoughts are rational and true. Seneca suggests that we do battle with ourselves. When you have the will to conquer anger it will become difficult for it to conquer you. Smile in the face of anger. Relax yourself and question it. Fight against the bodily movements and thought patterns of anger. Switch them to being calmer and happier.

Your opinion about something is what upsets you. Not the behaviors or the people. How much you value something determines the level of anger that comes from it. Think about it. Do you get upset by the same behaviors when it occurs in different contexts? For example, people being late. Or getting wet in the rain. Bear these value judgements in mind. Question whether they are really that important? Furthermore, question whether or not they are in your control.

Through self-reflection you can realize your ways of thinking and triggers for negative emotions. Practice some daily self-reflection to get in tune with what causes you anger and learn to slow it down. Seneca was a big advocate of self-reflection. He taught that our senses should be trained to make us stronger and durable. Marcus Aurelius understood that we should be aware of the circumstances which cause anger. Both would agree that we should reject anger and not be carried away by it. Like an enemy it must be met and driven back.

See yourself as the offender
Seneca advises that we see ourselves as the offender in angry confrontations with others.

When you get angry with someone, visualize yourself as them. Put yourself in their position. Is your anger still justified? Would you put up with how you're treating them? Is it acceptable behavior on your part? When you flip the script onto yourself the anger will quickly subside, and you can determine the correct way to proceed since you are coming at it from a mindset which is not clouded. Furthermore, if you have empathy for others, it will make you more tolerant of them. Maybe they are young or inexperienced. No one is perfect. All of us have our own flaws. Perhaps you have made the same mistakes before.

Marcus Aurelius took the view that everyone was doing their best and that they don't have ill will for others. The more tolerance you develop the more you can deal with personal conflicts. However, in developing tolerance it is important to not let people cross your boundaries or to take advantage of you. Always maintain healthy boundaries but at the same time have a higher threshold for not getting angry. All of this comes through experience. Staying calm when everyone else gets mad. When things go wrong it helps you continue to make good decisions which are not clouded by anger.

When we are hurt or wronged, we often want to take revenge. Prisons are based on this concept. Punishment for wrongdoing. However, people often come out of prison and offend again. Progressive countries are now starting to look at ways to heal rather than to punish. Now I'm not saying we should let people go without paying for the consequences of their actions. But the more we can let go of seeking revenge the better we can establish ourselves away from anger which fuels revenge. Seneca said that vengeance takes time and can expose one to more injuries and resentment. Catch yourself when you get caught up in that rage of revenge. Try to see the person in the whole picture. For whom they are.

For what kind of character, they have. Remember that everyone makes mistakes. Furthermore, remember to choose your friends carefully because anger is highly contagious. We become the average of people we associate with. If you're associating with negative angry people, then that will influence your behavior. It can be all too easy to be led astray and you don't want to get caught up in a mob. After all, you're only human. Cultivate relationships with people who are calm, honest, positive, tranquil and who have good self-control.

"Holding onto anger is like drinking poison and expecting the other person to die" - Seneca

The Toxic Emotion of Jealousy

Through the eyes of Stoicism jealousy is an illusion of permanence combined with believing that the external will make us happy. Realize that the universe is impermanent and that the external is outside of our control. When one is jealous, they wish not to lose something external and as such they attach themselves to it. Epictetus taught that we never own what we are attached to. The presence of it is temporary in our lives and in the blink of an eye we could lose it all. Understand that nothing lasts forever because one day you will ultimately be separated from it.

Now that doesn't mean you should be alone and have nothing to live for. Marcus Aurelius wrote that we shouldn't set our minds on what we don't possess. Instead, we ought to count our blessings for what we have and consider how much we might desire them if we didn't have them. Essentially, it's about making the most of what you have whilst you have it. Life changes constantly and change is the only constant. Resisting change makes us insecure. Jealousy arises from insecurity. We can never predict change, so it makes no sense to worry about trying to influence it or to worry about its influences. We can only do our best in this moment. The rest we have to embrace. Amor Fati reminds us to embrace and to love our fate.

Ultimately, we could put all of our efforts into relationships, status and possessions. But we can still lose them in an instant because ultimately you cannot truly control such externalities. In addition, they are also indifferents. Preferred indifferents that is but, in the end, they are still indifferent which means they aren't essential to your happiness. True happiness can be found in virtue which is to be free and not to be moved by misfortune.

Stop focusing on the external and switch your focus to the internal. Obsession over anything will eventually push it away from you. Live abundantly and freely. Incidentally when you focus on living in abundance instead of anxiety and clinging you will inevitably attract more people, moments and greatness into your life.

"Count the blessings you actually possess and think how much you would desire them if they weren't already yours." – Marcus Aurelius

The Toxic Emotion of Envy

Envy comes from social comparison. In our modern world we are surrounded by highlights of people being happy. Social media shows us just that, the highlights of someone's life. Naturally we assume that our life should be just as awesome. However, in reality, life is not a series of highlights. There is pain, struggle and a journey behind any life. All of which contribute to our growth and potential to become better. Chasing fleeting highlights will only lead to disappointment and guilt when you fall short of them.

Everyone has their own fortunes and starting points in life. Therefore, it is worthless to compare yourself to them or to be envious of them. But all too often we define ourselves in comparison to others. This is a powerful influence in how we conceptualize our own worth. When we feel inferior in some way you value whether it be beauty, wealth or so on then envy comes in. Ultimately envy is a reflection about how we feel about ourselves. When we are not smart enough, fit enough or beautiful enough and so on. Yet all of these are preferred indifferents and they are not in our control. Furthermore, they are impermanent and could disappear in an instant.

Lose your ego. Ego is a distorted view of one's significance and abilities. It is an unhealthy belief in how important one is. Ego leads to arrogance, recklessness and stubbornness. It stands in the way of what you want and could have. The ego is focused on being better than others. Don't focus on them. Focus on being your best. Stop comparing and showing off. Live your life and be your best. Live a life of virtue. Work without desire for recognition. The more you work against the ego the more it diminishes. Eventually you become more aligned with nature.

Envy is a poison of the mind. It puts a barrier between others and pushes you away from real connection with people. When people cling to thoughts of envy it causes them to practice immoral behaviors such as infidelity and criminal acts. But envy is not all bad. In fact, we can utilize it to improve ourselves as an inspiration to improve weaknesses. Think about some of your idols or inspirational things you have watched. Those probably make you feel small, but they also inspire you to become bigger and better.

So how does one overcome envy? First of all it requires self-awareness and examination. Become aware of your envy. Ask yourself why you are envious. Can you justify it? If you are envious of another person, realize that we all have different advantages in life. The pathway through envy is in being grateful for what you have. Focus on what you have and on making it better. That way you can only ever compare yourself to who you used to be and to who you are now. Instead of always seeking external validation and satisfaction look inwards. Realize that happiness is created from within your own mind. Outside events do not create it.

Stoicism can help you here to focus on what you have. It teaches us to be mindful of the present. To let go of energy spent living in the past or worrying about the future. Happiness and peace of mind come from within. They do not depend on the opinions of other people; they are all too important to give power over to someone else. Life is too short for that. Embrace the person you are and what makes you unique. Stop caring what others think. Go for what you want and be ruthless. Stop trying to please people and be someone you're not. Be you. In the cases where we desire something internal such as inner peace or happiness then it's a sign, we need to work more on ourselves. Pursuing virtue helps us to become stronger and to vanquish envy.

Marcus Aurelius the famous Stoic emperor wrote negatively about validation seeking behavior. This is enlightening for someone who would have been so famous in his time to write about. These days people are constantly seeking validation. Social media is prevalent and all about this. It has made the world imbalanced. People are praised for meaningless accomplishments and are gratified by likes, comments or follows. All this activates our dopamine happiness secreting chemicals which gives us temporary hits of pleasure. On the other hand, if we don't get it then we feel sad. Too many people are addicted to those hits and spend their lives chasing them. Whilst the world of love, joy and real social connections continue outside of their online bubble. Remember again that all of this is out of our control. With the rise of online connections, we are open to being viewed by much more people and judged by much more people. Maintain the same attitude of not caring what they think. Now that doesn't mean being arrogant. On the contrary you still act your best self and be a kind person but at the same time you let go of what people think of you. Face it not everyone will like you. No matter how much you try, some people just won't like you. Choose not to be hurt by the opinions of others. Choose to focus on your own mental well-being and be proud of who you are.

"Ambition means tying your well-being to

what other people say or do...Sanity means tying it to your own actions." - Marcus Aurelius

THE POWER OF NEGATIVE THINKING

The modern self-help industry tells us to think positively, encouraging us to be happy all day and to ignore any negative emotions. But without acknowledging pains and the negative emotions underlying then we are just glossing over deeper problems. Some studies have even shown that avoiding negative emotions only makes them stronger which can lead to much more stress later on. Essentially in avoiding negative emotions you are being dishonest with yourself. Often from places of pain, darkness and struggle is where we grow the most.

When we are comfortable with expressing negative emotions, it will help us become more comfortable with who we are. We can learn to understand ourselves better and have a deeper, true self love. Failure to recognize negative emotions or to pacify them with escape behaviors will never resolve the underlying problems. In fact, numerous studies have proven that the expression of negative emotions helps to build strong relationships. Don't escape and pacify your hurt with vices such as junk food or escapism. Give yourself some time out now and then but over the long-term focus on small daily improvements to dig yourself out of that hole and become your best self.

"A gem cannot be polished without friction, nor a man perfected without trials." – Seneca

Premeditatio Malorum

Stoicism encourages us to expect that things will

go wrong. Premeditatio Malorum or "the premeditation of evils" is a mental exercise taught in Stoicism to help students imagine the worst possible scenarios of what could happen to them. According to Stoicism we should be ready for challenges and adversity. They are inevitable and so we should consider everything that could possibly go wrong. Think about it. What are the challenges you could face and what would you do about them? Those who can thrive in the hard times are able to do so by focusing on what they can control to make the situation better. Seneca believed that by doing this exercise he would be prepared for any fate that he might meet with. Incidentally he faced many adversities in his life including being exiled as a prisoner for many years. Through each adversity he persevered with strength, bravery and understanding. Victory and defeat he dealt with equally.

The goal of Premeditatio Malorum is to help one

prepare for life's adversities and uncertainties because things won't always go to plan as we hope they will. Therefore, we need to build a strong psychological foundation to help prepare us for when things go wrong. The more we prepare the further we can go. Positive thinking will get you started but you also need some cynicism to ensure you go all the way. For example, think of what it takes to start a business. If you were overly optimistic you might run out of cash too soon. However, with a bit of Premeditatio Malorum you would realize that running out of money is likely to happen. As such you would prepare accordingly and be able to run through any dip that might happen. Furthermore, if it doesn't happen more strength to you!

"Rehearse them in your mind: exile, torture, war, shipwreck. All the terms of our human lot should be before our eyes." - Seneca

Consider any goal or upcoming event you have in mind and apply this strategy to it. What's the worst that could happen? How would you overcome that? Your answers should give you some clear-cut plans in the event of any tragedy occurring. Now hopefully that doesn't happen but, in any case, you should be prepared. Tim Ferriss, the bestselling author came up with his own version of Premeditatio Malorum and he called it "fear setting". There are four steps to fear setting.

Step one: Write down whatever it is you are not confident about doing. Maybe that is applying for a new job, going on a date or traveling to a new place.

Step two: Write down what your worries of things that could go wrong are. Maybe you could get a rejection. Maybe things don't go to plan, or you screw up.

Step three: Write down what you would do if these worst-case scenarios actually happened. How would you overcome them?

Step four: Write down what the best-case scenarios could be. What is the best that could happen?

Through completing this exercise, you will often realize that the worst-case scenarios aren't really that bad. Plus, you will be more ready for them if they do happen. In fact, often you will see that actions are worth taking that risk to achieve the best-case scenarios. Eventually you will become comfortable with those results and understand how you would overcome them. Follow the four steps of fear setting anytime you are facing a challenge.

"I may wish to be free from torture, but if the time comes for me to endure it, I'll wish to bear it courageously with bravery and honor."– Seneca

Practicing misfortune

In modern times we experience a comfortable quality of life. A warm bed, food in the fridge and a roof over our heads. Whether you consider yourself lucky or not you're probably better off than most people in the world. Certainly, more so than over two thousand years ago. However, being in such comfort we often forget how fortunate our circumstances are. But what if we didn't have such comforts?

Practicing misfortune is an exercise the ancient Stoics used to help them appreciate the comforts they had. In order to practice misfortune, one goes about giving up some of their comforts for a short period of time. The theory behind it is that we carry anxiety and doubts about losing what we have which holds us back from taking risks to become better. However, if we practice living as if we lost that which we fear losing then it makes us stronger and more comfortable with taking risks towards growth. Furthermore, it makes us more grateful for what we have.

Consider how you could practice misfortune. Maybe you eat the same meal every day for a week. Or you live in a basic apartment for a month. Or you sleep on the floor for a week. Imagine you lost all your money. As a result, you would have to live much more frugally. Try it out and see how it would feel for you. Probably you will realize that it's not all that bad. I once went to live with monks for a few days where I slept on the floor of a wooden hut in the forest. Yet during that time I slept so well. In conclusion of the experience, I realized that if everything went wrong in my life I could come and live there. I was ok with that. In fact, I was happy there free from materialism and attachments.

Seneca himself said that each month we should set aside some days to practice poverty. Have a little food, wear cheap clothes and escape from your comforts. Then ask yourself "Is this what I really dread?". Comfort can make you a slave and keep you trapped from the life you truly want. Prepare yourself and make yourself comfortable with being uncomfortable. Not only will it make you stronger it will also give you more confidence to take those risks towards rewards.

In addition to building more mental toughness it's wise to build a strong body. The ancient Stoics advised their students to practice cold exposure and fasting because they knew that too much comfort is a weakness. Seneca, who was a rich man, practiced fasting and was often underdressed for cold weather. Fasting and cold exposure are great for health. Science has found that they can strengthen immunity and make us more tolerant to pain. In addition, we should also implement a weekly exercise regime.

Work on having the best health you can. Take care of your body. Eat healthy food and do not overindulge. Get into a regular exercise routine. Make sure you get plenty of sleep. Cut out any things which negatively affect your health. To live your best life, it helps to have a healthy body and mind. The better care you take of your health the more life you have to enjoy. You live longer and function better. Lift weights and build strength. Run and improve your cardiovascular system. Eat healthy and clean. These habits will build you a healthy and strong body. A body that can handle a strong mind. A body that can deal with stress and fight for a better life.

Memento Mori

One last thing on negative thinking! Meditate on death to bring clarity to your life. We will all die one day. In fact during our lifetime, we will die many times. The child dies to become an adult. The single man dies to become a husband and so on. Our existence is fragile. Think about where you were five years ago. How quickly did that time pass? Imagine how quickly the next five years will pass. Life could stop at any moment, and you never know when that moment might be. Accepting death is a life philosophy we should all practice.

When we die, we return back to a state of nonexistence. One day you are going to die. There is no escaping that. Acknowledging this will help you to waste less time on the things that are not important. Indeed, life can be long enough to do what matters. But it is still short enough to waste. Ultimately time cannot be taken back. Allow this to drive the actions you take and let it motivate you to spend your time more wisely. Don't think about this as all doom and gloom. But rather as a way to motivate you to be more specific, purposeful and meaningful in the way you live. Remind yourself that time is your most precious commodity.

"It's not that we have a short time to live, but that we waste a lot of it." –Seneca

Ultimately, we cannot be truly alive whilst we are consumed by fears and the ultimate fear, death. The philosophy of Memento Mori which is the Stoic contemplation of death helps one to be fearless in the face of death. The ancient Stoics were well aware of their mortality. Life is short and they realized that death was coming to them one day. Death is outside of our control and so we should remain indifferent to it. When one becomes sad and overwhelmed by death one must realize that it is their impression or judgment of the event which distresses them. Death doesn't have to be a bad thing. Only when you associate that judgment to it. See life as a temporary thing and allow that to motivate you to excel.

For those of us who have come close to death we can understand how much it makes you prioritize what is important in life. For most we realize what our true values are. Understand that externals such as wealth and reputation cannot be taken with us to the grave. To accept our death helps us to rise above petty troubles. Stoicism calls this magnanimity which is to have a big soul and a vast mind. Magnanimity helps one to rise above everything. When one can accept the certainty of their death then they are on the way to Stoic magnanimity. They are on the way to expanding beyond their troubles. To be free of pain and pleasure.

Every night Seneca reminded himself that he might not awaken to live the next day. Marcus Aurelius constantly contemplated his own death, imagining himself to be already dead and living on borrowed time. Such contemplation helps one to realize that most worries in life are trivial. Too often we run away from the facts of life. Instead, we need to face them head on. Indeed, it might seem dark and depressing to meditate on your mortality. However, on the contrary it can be utilized as a tool to understand meaning and priority. To make one realize what is important and what is not. To make us use our time on earth wisely and to not waste it. This brings us closer to living the life we want to live. Don't be the one who finds out they have months to live and then start a bucket list. Live now!

"Those whom you love and those whom you

despise will both be made equal in the same ashes" - *Seneca*

PRINCIPLES FOR INNER PEACE & HAPPINESS

Happiness is what makes us uniquely human. Other animals don't experience such kinds of emotions. The definition of happiness is to be cheerful and to have enjoyable experiences. Most people associate it with external factors which are largely out of our control. For example, being healthy, rich or having a stable family. Stoicism teaches us that if you live in the right way then happiness will result. We have covered this before, which is to live in alignment with nature. We are therefore responsible for our own happiness. Any external thing that we might think brings us happiness is really something indifferent. Whether that is wealth, health, social status, material possessions and so on.

The ancient Stoics realized that happiness depends on your own efforts and qualities. Virtue and the qualities of character are critical to this. Developing our virtue and character, wisdom, courage, justice and moderation depends on us. Essentially if you live according to the virtues, you will be happy. According to Stoicism we can be happy without possession of externals because they do not make a difference between being happy or sad. Indeed, it is possible to live a good life without them. As long as you exercise the virtues.

When we experience negative emotions, it is usually based on a false judgment that some external thing is good or bad. When we lose something, we think has value it causes us sadness. Or when we associate happiness with something fleeting. Good emotions are more consistent and longer lasting. When we can learn to accept our fate and non-permanent view of life we can detach from those externals and live in alignment with nature.

Almost two thousand years ago ancient Stoic philosophers set out on their journeys to find inner peace and happiness. They created practices and rituals to cultivate inner peace and happiness. To this day all of us want peace of mind. For some of us it is easier said than done. These days life is moving so fast. We are in a rush from the moment we wake up. Social media and entertainment keep us distracted in those moments of boredom and tiredness. But in those moments, we need to search for stillness. Take time for your mind to unwind and to do nothing. If you're not allowing your mind to do that then you will probably struggle to sleep at night. In bed your mind races and processes the day's events. Don't let that happen. Instead during the day let your mind unwind naturally. Take time out for short walks, journaling or just chilling out.

Gratitude

Gratitude is the foundation of a happier and stronger mind. Stoicism teaches us that wanting less will increase gratitude whilst wanting more will reduce it. In psychology this is known as hedonic adaptation. When we are grateful, we transition from those feelings of lack or not having what we want. Essentially it breaks the cycle of wanting and needing. Furthermore, it can break you free from jealousy and envy. When one is grateful for what they have they desire less and as a result they feel happier with what they have now. The ancient Stoics were focused on reducing the desire of wanting more and in turn cultivating more gratitude. When we let go of pursuing or wanting more and fearing what we may lose it frees us to be in the present moment. Epictetus called gratitude 'eucharistos' which is the art of seeing the truth of what is happening in each moment.

Imagine the farmer in a poor rural village versus the high-powered corporate executive. Who do you think is happier? Probably the farmer because he is grateful for having what he has, a family around him and a simple life. Whilst the executive is always chasing desire. Yes, it is good to have goals to go for. But more stuff won't necessarily make you happier. Appreciation of it will make you happy and gratitude is the key to that. Realize how lucky you are to be living in this world. The very fact that you're here and living is a miracle in itself. Stoicism teaches us to be aware of our mortality in order to be grateful for the shortness of life. Don't let the small stuff get you down. Meditate on the big picture and on the uniqueness of you being here. Be present to the moment. Focus on the here and now. Forget about your worries or regrets. Most of the time we worry about things that never even end up happening.

"When you arise in the morning, think of what a precious privilege it is to be alive."

– Marcus Aurelius

Accept your fate and be grateful for literally everything, including the bad stuff. Be grateful for everything that happens to you because it is all part of the universe's grand scheme. Furthermore, it is not just about being personally grateful but for the whole of our universe. We should also seek and celebrate the advancement of our friends as much as we do for ourselves. This is living in alignment with nature. True it's not easy to be grateful for those setbacks, bad experiences and so on. But it is all possible. For example, maybe that failed relationship led you to the love of your life. Or maybe losing your job led to you starting a business. Often, we are just one step away from our destiny. See every perceived set back as a step closer. Focus on the positive things in your life. Even though some things might not work out your way, it's all about perspective. Realize that in the big picture you're still here and living. Realize that every bad situation often has a silver lining. All that happens to you is for the reason to shape who you are and bring you to where you need to be. Understanding this will help you to become more grateful.

Practicing gratitude

Practicing gratitude is important because it doesn't come by itself. It needs to be cultivated. All of us are born on different points of happiness. Gratitude has been proven many times to raise that. Make an intentional choice to be grateful and happy for everything. The ancient Stoics believed in being grateful for what we have in life and never taking anything for granted or to never complain. Complaining only keeps you in an ungrateful state which hurts you. Again, it is useless because it's focused on the past which cannot be changed. Learn from the past. Don't live there. Put your energy into having a better present and future. Quit complaining because it archives nothing. Accept that you cannot change the world or the people in it.

"He is wise who doesn't grieve for the things he doesn't have but rejoices for the things he does have." – Epictetus

Journaling

According to the Harvard Business School journaling is a proven way to increase gratitude, performance, manage stress and gain clearer thinking. Try keeping a gratitude journal where you can write about all the things, you're grateful for. This practice will help you to cultivate more gratitude in your life. Every morning I like to write down at least ten things I am grateful for. They can be anything, from the small to the big things. For example, the air I breathe or for having my family. I like to write them all down. Everyday it's different. Just ask yourself what you're grateful for today and let your pen flow. Think about how they make you feel. Practice this during the day in your mind also. In fact, anytime you feel down it can be a powerful antidote.

Marcus Aurelius the great Stoic and Roman emperor wrote one of the most famous journals in history, Meditations. It was his private journal which after his death became public knowledge. Those minutes he spent alone each day with his journal helped to turn him into one of the greatest men to ever live in the world. The miracle of his journal surviving almost two thousand years proves its value. Reflecting on one's thoughts onto paper was a common practice back then. Each person has their own way of journaling. The purpose of Stoic journaling is not necessarily about recording your own history. You can also use it to reflect on your life or to work things out. Or maybe just to clear your head and to solve the mental issues you have going on. For Marcus Aurelius the purpose of journaling was to remind himself of how to live a virtuous life.

Stoicism says that we have control over our inner world. Through introspection, self-awareness and gratitude we can become our best self. Reflect on your life. Acknowledge your negative and positive sides. Work on them. Continue to grow and develop inner strength with journaling. Make the time for it. Sacrifice some of your texting and social media time. Wake up in the morning and use your journal to write about whatever is on your mind at that time. Also, throughout the day you will be likely to have some ideas or important things come up. Make a note of them. This could be on your phone note pad to make it easier to record. The more you do this the more capacity your brain has to be inventive. Sometimes the best ideas come completely out of the blue. Make sure you take a note of them. Or at the end of the day take some time to reflect on it. What went well? What didn't go well? How could you have made it better? Let it flow out onto the paper. Don't hold back. Consider it like a kind of private therapy. Remember that path to greatness comes from self-reflection and awareness.

Allow yourself to write whatever you feel. There are no rules so don't censor yourself. Use it to consult with yourself, make better decisions and to gain clarity of mind. Free your mind to live life in the present moment. Allow the darkest secrets, fears, anxieties, dreams and whatever to come out. Start with just writing in the morning for five minutes or so. Maybe you could answer a few prompts such as what you're grateful for or what's currently a challenge for you. It doesn't need to be outstanding grammar and perfect writing. Just start writing and let it flow. Stream of conscious journaling is one of the most useful ways to relieve stress and become happier. Let your thoughts flow onto the paper.

Think of some of the most important questions you ask yourself. Perhaps those are questions such as. Why do I want to be rich? How can I become rich? What kind of relationship do I want? Who brings out the best in me? How can I become a better person? What am I grateful for? And so on. Have them written in your journal as writing triggers. You could do these in the morning, evening or when it is suitable. Write out what your goals are. Those can be your vision, long term and in the short term. Write them out in detail. Brainstorm how to get there.

What you need. Take inventory and map it out. Bring it all into your awareness.

CONCLUSION

Stoicism is about conquering yourself and it gives us a blueprint by which we can live our best lives. Think of it like a life code which gives you answers to questions and ways of how to conduct yourself. When we embrace it, we can be free from so much of the mental activity that tires us out. Some might think this a restrictive way of living but for the ancient Stoics they believed it released them from anxiety and uncertainty. In turn this brings us peace and a path to follow. Now let us conclude this book by going over what we have learned on our journey.

We began this book by talking about the problems of modern society. Now more than ever it has become fragmented and disconnected. We are lost and seeking answers to why our life doesn't match the ideal portrayed in the media. False illusions convince us that we need more things to be happy. Maybe, more wealth, materialism and love are the answers. Yet we end up in lonely pursuits disconnected from our true nature. Looking for answers we get lost in all the endless stream of gurus and self-help or we act selfishly in the pursuit of our solo endeavors. Ancient Stoics over two thousand years ago realized that happiness doesn't come from the material possessions around us. They understood that events are not inherently good or bad. Our mind is what decides upon that. Status symbols such as wealth and fame are indeed preferred to their opposite, but they are not essential to living a good life. As long as one has the right frame of mind then they can live well regardless of most circumstances.

Stoicism was developed as a way to help people live their best lives. Yet many people have avoided it because they think that they will require them to turn off their emotions or that they will not be allowed any more pleasures. Well that as we have seen in this book is just not the truth. What we have discovered is that you don't need to follow any religious practices, and neither will you need to throw away all your possessions or live isolated from society. However, living the way of a Stoicism is going to require a personal reinvention. In doing so the promise of this life is tranquility, to deal with negative emotions more effectively and in turn have a stronger character who is living their best life.

At the beginning of this book, we explored the origins of Stoicism. This is important to understand because it paints a full picture of where it came from and who the famous philosophers from ancient history were. We can understand their minds and what was going on in their lives at that time it was created. The golden age. Indeed, they also suffered many of the anxieties and problems that we now face. Again, that's why Stoicism is such a timeless philosophy.

Moving on we took a look at the foundations of Stoicism. The universe guides and connects all of us together. Think of it as being God in everything. When one considers themself in isolation from the universe then they're going to suffer in misery. When one realizes that one is part of the universe, they can start to make decisions that live in alignment with nature and that is a virtuous life. Goodness comes from understanding our place in the universe and collaborating with it for all of our benefit. This is the foundation of Stoicism which is living virtuously. Happiness is a by-product of this way of living.

To further explain the foundations of Stoicism we took a look at the happiness triangle consisting of Eudaimonia at the center which is the goal of life. Essentially it means to flourish. Connected to it on the triangle are to "Live with Arete" which is to become your best self. That requires developing your character to the highest levels and closing the gap between who you are now and who your best self is. The other points on that triangle are to take responsibility for everything in your life and to be aware of what you control.

In the next chapter we explored virtue which is the true pathway to happiness. To live virtuously we need to be aware of the four cardinal virtues which are wisdom, temperance, justice and moderation. At the opposite end is vice which brings negativity whilst in the middle are gray indifferents which don't necessarily contribute to happiness. Rather they are just preferred or not prefered. When we misjudge them is when we evaluate something as being more than what is necessary for happiness. Regardless of our background one can live virtuously and that will be its own reward. If you struggle with living virtuously, ask yourself questions in any situation you are facing. Pass them through the four cardinals to determine whether it's worthwhile for you to take action or to avoid that situation.

Moving on we explored the dichotomy of control which is one of the most popular teachings of Stoicism. In summary life can be divided into what we control and what we don't control. Realize that there is very little you control and when you try to control what you cannot become emotionally disturbed by it. Ultimately what you really do control is your internal world. Focus on this and leave the rest in God's hands. Stoicism calls this Amor Fati, which is the love of fate. We must love whatever comes to us because it's not in our power. Focus on what you control, which is your internal world, let go of the rest and accept your fate.

In the next chapter we explored desires. Since the beginning of time desires have led us astray. All too often they have led to unhealthy passions, compulsions and obsessions. According to Stoicism a human consumed by desire is akin to a human acting as an animal. Realize that there are so many temptations and desires coming at us all the time. Therefore, we must take responsibility for not being led astray. Often, we need to delay gratification, and, in this chapter, we explored how to do that effectively. We looked at keyways for dealing with temptations that can lead us astray.

Stoicism suggests the concept of Apatheia which

is the mind-state free from emotional disturbance. Again, this isn't about depriving yourself. Instead, it guides one to divide passions into unhealthy and healthy. A well-trained Stoic understands the difference. Seneca said we should enjoy pleasures that come to us, to act reasonably with them and to not overindulge. Of course, everything in moderation is fine. But we must also remain indifferent to them because one day we will lose them.

Moving forward we explored emotions. Again, I'm highlighting here that Stoicism is not the suppression of emotions. Mastery of emotions is the goal here and to not be carried away by them. In this chapter we explored how to gain mastery of your emotions and their inner workings. We took a look at the three stages of emotions which are stimulus, perception and response. Understanding these three stages identifies the gap between stimulus to perception and response. We're all affected by stimulus, whoever we are. Ultimately that's up to nature and you can't change that. However, we have the ability of applying reason to look at our perceptions objectively and then to determine the right course of response which aligns with nature.

Additionally in exploring emotions we dived deep into the toxic emotions namely anger, stress, jealousy and envy. We took a deep dive into those emotions to understand what they are and how to deal with them effectively. Stoicism works very well here because those emotions were studied thoroughly by ancient stoics. Again, it's a timeless philosophy which has worked on humans for thousands of years. In reality these negative emotions are based on incorrect judgements which lead us to unpleasant experiences and actions. As Seneca said they are "a temporary madness" and should be avoided at all costs because all too often they lead us to bad endings.

In the later chapters we explored the power of negative thinking, positivity and happiness. I understand that many of you are going to be put off about thinking negatively. However, you must realize that negative emotions will often bring you improvement as you rise from those places of darkness and struggle. Acknowledge them instead of glossing over them. Then you can draw strength from them. The ancient Stoics were well aware of this, and they had some specific practices or negative thinking exercises which were outlined in this chapter.

Premeditatio Malorum is to negatively visualize all the wrong things that could happen to us. Use this exercise for upcoming situations that you might have anxiety about. Determine all the things that could go wrong and how you would deal with them. Furthermore, envision all the best things that could happen. The practice will reveal that it's not so bad which will probably motivate you to go ahead and take action.

Next, we explored how the Stoics practice misfortune. Essentially this is to put ourselves in uncomfortable situations for a short period of time. Become comfortable with the uncomfortable and it will make you stronger when faced with adversity. Death is a guarantee of life. Sorry to be so negative but there is no escaping that fact. Memento Mori is the old famous Stoic concept of meditating on your death. Accepting that one day you will day will help you to appreciate and make the most of your life. Furthermore, accept the mortality of your friends and family. Let that motivate you to make the most of your time with them. Make peace with accepting your mortality. I know that sounds very dark and dreadful but it's in fact a great way to look at the shortness of life. Allow that to motivate you and to not waste time.

In the final chapter we explored positivity and happiness which of course is what we all want. Now that all depends on your efforts and living virtuously. When you live according to nature it is a virtuous way of living which will in turn make you happy. We explored here that gratitude is the foundation of a happy and strong mind. We need to be grateful for what we have. When we want less it will increase our gratitude. Whilst wanting more makes us needy and unhappy. Transition from those feelings of want or not having.

Stoicism teaches us to be grateful for literally everything including the bad experiences because in the grand scheme we are still living. Right now, we don't know if those bad experiences are really good or not. Maybe in the long run they will lead us towards something better. Therefore, we need to cultivate more gratitude. Journaling is a great way of bringing into your awareness of what you are already grateful for. Marcus Aurelius wrote one of the most famous journals. In it he explored his gratitude and reflected on his life. Self-reflection is the key to improving oneself.

Marcus Aurelius was the emperor of Rome. He likely had access to unlimited luxury. But he did not obsess over luxury. He was a wise man who found beauty in simplicity. Noting that simple things are beautiful in their own unique way. Take a look at the sky for example and be humbled by it. Walk out in nature and take it all in.

Stoicism teaches us that the universe is a vast and unexplained place. We are humans who need to appreciate our place in it. Remember that the foundation of Stoicism is the universe that we are all connected through. Living in alignment with nature is all about understanding our place in the universe. We have to realize that we're all connected together like a large entity. Our life should encompass the greater good of humanity because that is a virtuous way of living. Ultimately this requires an assent to providence. Essentially that is to be guided by God.

Inside of us we all have a personal God and when we let our characters turn bad, giving into the devil inside then negative events occur. That is the real demon of life. Indeed, it is often easier said than done. When those external distractions and desires come up it can be at times difficult to say no. Take care of your fellow humans to lift them up and to do good things for them. Yes, this seems like a lot of responsibility but when you act that way it's going to be virtuous. Happiness will be a byproduct of it. Help people to become better including becoming a better person yourself because it will lift up our society.

Thousands of years ago the Stoics figured a way of living with less suffering and more enjoyment. At its core Stoicism is a philosophy for happiness. Living a meaningful and happy life is the deepest desire of humans. We want to feel important and connected in the world. We want to be proud of the life we are living. Ultimately, we want to live our best life. We want to share that life with the people we love. Living your best life requires being your best self. Life is a journey of ups and downs. We all know this. Stoicism will help you to ride through it all. It will help you to be capable of experiencing both pleasure and pain without them causing ruin.

Seneca reminds us through his letters that alongside the pursuit of virtue we should strive for something meaningful in our life. Our focus should be on cultivating a mind of excellence. This requires us to pay attention to the judgments we make and to develop positive character traits such as wisdom, courage, moderation and justice. These virtues will help us to become better people and to live in alignment with nature. The only true good is to have a virtuous character and a rational mind. This as the Stoics would say is the requirement of living a good life.

I wish you all the best on your journey to living The Way of The Stoic. Please revisit this book again and again to refresh the philosophy of Stoicism in your mind. Now if you would please kindly take the time to leave a review of this book where you purchased it.

Thank you and good luck my friend.

REFERENCES

Aurelius, M., & Hammond, M. (2006). Meditations (Penguin Classics). Penguin Classics.

E., & Dobbin, R. (2008). Discourses and Selected Writings (Penguin Classics) (1st ed.). Penguin Classics.

E., & Long, G. (2004). Enchiridion (Dover Thrift Editions: Philosophy) (unknown ed.). Dover Publications.

Ferriss, T. (2009). The 4-Hour Workweek: Escape 9–5, Live Anywhere, and Join the New Rich (Expanded, Updated ed.). Harmony.

Graham, S. M., Huang, J. Y., Clark, M. S., & Helgeson, V. S. (2008). The Positives of Negative Emotions: Willingness to Express Negative Emotions Promotes

Relationships. Personality and Social Psychology Bulletin, 34(3), 394–406. https://doi.org/10.1177/0146167207311281

Harvard Health. (2011, October 11). Writing about emotions may ease stress and trauma. https://www.health.harvard.edu/healthbeat/writing-about-emotions-may-ease-stress-and-trauma

Why 'bottling it up' can be harmful to your health | HCF. (2018). HEALTH AGENDA. https://www.hcf.com.au/health-agenda/body-mind/mental-health/downsides-to-always-being-positive#:%7E:text=And%20avoiding%20emotions%20can%20also,re%20actually%20making%20them%20stronger.

Hendel, H. J. (2018, February 27). Ignoring Your Emotions Is Bad for Your Health.

Here's What to Do About It. Time. https://time.com/5163576/ignoring-your-emotions-bad-for-your-health/

Irvine, W. B. (2008). A Guide to the Good Life: The Ancient Art of Stoic Joy (1st ed.). Oxford University Press.

Irvine, W. B. (2007). On Desire: Why We Want What We Want (New Ed). Oxford University Press.

Laertius, D., & Hicks, R. D. (1925). Diogenes Laertius: Lives of Eminent Philosophers, Volume I, Books 1–5 (Loeb Classical Library No. 184). Harvard University Press.

Seneca, L. A., & Campbell, R. (1969). Letters from a Stoic (Penguin Classics) (Reprint ed.). Penguin Books.

Stoic Week 2018 part 3. (2021, September 10). Modern Stoicism. https://modernstoicism.com/report/sto

ic-week-2018-part-3/

Start Your Week The Right Way

We've all had that sinking feeling on a Sunday night, when you remember it's Monday tomorrow and the weekend is over. It can be tricky trying to launch ourselves back into work-mode, but with the right motivation and mentality, you can get your week off to the perfect start.

Receive evidence-based guidance, up-to-date resources, and first-hand accounts to help you.

Sign Up Now & You will receive this newsletter every Monday.

https://www.subscribepage.com/tswain

Scan the QR code to join.

OTHER BOOKS BY THOMAS SWAIN

Way of The Spartan

Way of The Spartan (eBook)

Way of The Spartan (audiobook)

Overthinking

Overthinking (eBook)

Overthinking (audiobook)

Branding

Branding (eBook)

Branding (audiobook)

www.ingramcontent.com/pod-product-compliance
Lightning Source LLC
Chambersburg PA
CBHW071614080526
44588CB00010B/1130